CORREZE

BRIVE

Montignac

Turenne

Collonges

Cressensac

Beaulieu

Salignac
Barrèze
Souillac
Cazoules

Martel

Vayrac

Bretenoux
CHÂTEAU
CASTELNAU

Les Eyzies

SARLAT

Creysse
St Sozy

Carennac
Meyronne
Padirac

St Céré

Beynac

CHÂTEAU FENELON

Lacave

Alvignac

CHÂTEAU
MONTAL

Domme

Paysac

Cales

Rocamadour

Gramat

Gourdon

Gabrerets

CAHORS

SCALE

miles.

0   12½   25

SOUILLAC
& ENVIRONS

AN UNFINISHED JOURNEY

The Prophet Isaiah, Abbey Church of Souillac

AN UNFINISHED JOURNEY

JOURNEY

To South-Western France and Auvergne

By

PETER de POLNAY

LONDON

ALLAN WINGATE

12 Beauchamp Place, S.W.3

First published 1952
ALLAN WINGATE (PUBLISHERS) LTD
12 Beauchamp Place, London S.W.3

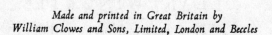

Made and printed in Great Britain by
William Clowes and Sons, Limited, London and Beccles

CONTENTS

ACKNOWLEDGEMENTS

I am deeply grateful to Dr. Andrew Geddes-Brown for the use of his photographs of Souillac facing pages 6, 7 and 28, of Roc-Amadour facing pages 36 and 37, of Turenne facing page 37 and of the Dordogne Valley facing page 136; to Dr. Cany for his photographs of the Virgin of Auvergne facing page 137, of Vic-sur-Cère facing page 152, and of the Viaduct of Garabit facing page 201; and to Monsieur Pierre Betz for the frontispiece and the photograph of the Souillac Tympanum facing page 153. The photograph of faire chabrol *facing page 29 was supplied by Monsieur Robert Doisneau, and the remaining subjects by the London office of the* Commissariat Général au Tourisme.

P. de P.

LIST OF ILLUSTRATIONS

TO

NADA PATCEVITCH

Chapter One

SOUILLAC

I

"AUVERGNE," I said to my wife Margaret, and the Mediterranean was blue; the Mistral whipped it, blowing lumbago, rheumatism, colds and pneumonia into the bay of Nice. The mountains glittered, as if they were in the window of an expensive shop. "Auvergne," I said again, and we walked towards the perennially picturesque market of Antibes. I had never been to Auvergne, yet for some obscure reason it captured my imagination. It was an unknown, uncharted land which even many of my French friends didn't know, a country with one-way traffic only; for the Auvergnat often leaves Auvergne, but few strangers penetrate his world of extinct volcanoes, rivers and lakes. The cradle of Lafayette and Laval, the enforced home of the Reine Margot; and we walked on with the Mistral behind us. A car came at enormous speed. A fat dog detached himself, as it were, from the wall of a house facing the harbour, then rushed into the road. There was a heavy thump: it took the driver some time to stop the car.

"Whose dog is this?" asked the driver when he got out.

He should have said: whose dog was this? The dog lay dead in the middle of the road. His number, whichever way you looked at it, was up. A small crowd had already gathered with the speed the occasion called for. The dog's owner was nowhere; somebody said he had belonged to a widow, and the bespectacled, obese driver was deeply moved. Somebody else said the dog had had no road sense:

last Sunday he had nearly been run over by a motor cycle. The driver said that was still no excuse for the dog to have met such a tragic end. The poor widow; and he shook his head. Eventually he bowed to the dead dog and drove away. My dog Jamie had already moved on with my wife. If I hear Auvergne mentioned I see the fat dog lying in the road, the Mistral blows, and the sky is of an icy deep blue.

"Not a good omen for Auvergne," said my wife. I pointed out, however, that I didn't want to stay much longer in the South of France.

During the war years I had longed for the South of France: in the black-out, in Nissen huts, in battledress and in overcrowded dark railway compartments, and tried to imagine the Alpes Maritimes somewhere above the barrage balloons, and made the insipid joke that the war was being fought for the Route Nationale No. 7. The war ended, a few more years went by, and when we arrived in the autumn of 1948 at the station of Nice I knew that something had gone utterly wrong. Probably I had waited too long; possibly I had changed too much and couldn't return to the days preceding the outbreak of the last war. The blue of sky and sea seemed too theatrical, hence insincere, the ugly bungalows, with which the coast was littered, weren't there perhaps before the war—or I hadn't noticed them.

"Let us go to Auvergne," I said three months after our arrival.

"The dead dog," said my wife. Besides, it was the beginning of February, and snow and cold would be lying heavily on Auvergne.

It wasn't only a case of the ugly bungalows, most of which bore the name of Oustalou: it was a case of the residents, that is the British residents, many of whom had remained behind during the war. One finds disillusioned people who say the war has been fought in vain, but brushing

2

other considerations aside, the conspicuous fact sticks out that the chasm can't be bridged between those who were in the war and those who were not. The local population, occupied by the not unfriendly Italians, hadn't suffered a great deal either; and taking it all in all I felt as if I were moving among men and women brought up on different lines. Or to speak more in harmony with local colour, I was at a cocktail party where unknown drinks were served, and the conversation was in an unknown language, a language I had no desire to learn.

What with the dead dog and the winter in Auvergne, it was difficult to think of some other place to go. A few days later I went to London. I asked a friend, a man intimately acquainted with France, to suggest some district which wasn't cold yet had nothing in common with the Riviera.

"Souillac," he said. I asked him to repeat the name.

"Is it cold?" I asked.

"Never really cold," he said, "and you'll be able to work there."

I was willing to believe him that it wasn't really cold in Souillac, but for a writer to believe that anybody but himself could know where he would be able to work was another matter. At any rate, I thanked him and went to lunch with Palinurus, who had written of the Magic Circle. I put my problem to him.

"Souillac," he said. For Souillac is in the Magic Circle, and that somehow clinched it.

I returned to Antibes. During the night in the overheated sleeping-car I felt the cold, snowbound winter running with the train. The more unbearably hot it became in the train, the colder it was outside. Somewhere south of Avignon the winter lost the race and fell back, I imagine, panting. In Marseilles, as I had done many times before, I stood on the platform and watched the uncoupling of the first two sleepers, which go only as far as Marseilles. On another line the breakfast-car was waiting. A voice said through the loudspeaker: "Attention à la manœuvre," and a little engine first disposed of the sleepers, that is pulled them to the remise, then rushed the breakfast-car to the train. The early morning sky was a canopy for lovers, a few white clouds were fired by the sun, the air was still and pleasantly tepid: the air the gods had cherished. I began to waver; for I could think of no sky comparable to the sky of the Mediterranean. But soon the crop of oustalous was picked out by the sun. In the breakfast-car I sat at a table with a large, evidently rich Frenchman who told me that Marshal Pétain alone could save France. Later he spoke of the pleasures of the years of occupation. I wavered no more.

When I make up my lazy mind I make it up quickly. I had already telegraphed my wife asking her to pack and be ready to leave. She and my dog Jamie were at the station of Antibes. I said we were off to Souillac. It was her turn to ask me to repeat the name. The Mistral wasn't blowing and it was stuffy: the rain wouldn't be long in coming. In the evening I went to the Municipal Casino in Cannes. The days of the end of the black market were still in the offing. Rapacious hands clung to plaques bought with the proceeds of dollars and butter. An inspector came up to me, said there was an empty place at the big chemin de fer table, but with one foot already on the road to Souillac, I said I wasn't gambling. He turned his back on me. That was my good-bye to the South of France. Next afternoon we took train to Marseilles.

Marseilles plays an unaccountable role in my life. I always expect to meet it, so to speak, round the corner; and seldom fail to. First I had known Marseilles as a port. I sailed from Marseilles to South America; I took ship from Marseilles to Kenya. On such occasions Marseilles was an inspiring point of departure. I rushed round and saw little, my mood expansive because a new life was beginning. The great thing about a new life is the beginning—hence wedding breakfasts. Then I came to know Marseilles as a port of arrival: I came in a small cargo boat from Tunis and went to spend two years on the Riviera. The next time I met Marseilles was in the autumn of 1940 and I became acquainted with it from behind prison bars—but of that I have written elsewhere. In 1947 Marseilles once more became the first chapter of a journey: my wife and I left Marseilles in a rusty Greek ship to spend the winter on the delectable island of Cyprus.

Now we arrived in Marseilles in the evening. Again Marseilles played its old part. It became the pillar of the unfinished journey of which Souillac is the post.

For one who knows Marseilles comparatively well it is difficult to become accustomed to the disappearance of the Pont Transbordeur, a horrible contraption, yet it had been part and parcel of the town. The burned-out Old Port creates a void too, in spite of the salubrious effect it must have on local morals. It is difficult to accept the once famous restaurants as decaying expensive eating houses; that, however, is the case. Much of the town's vitality and gaiety went with the war and with the gradual liquidation of the British Empire. The continuous stream of civil servants on furlough from the Empire is practically over. The Cannebière is quiet, the cafés not too full. Perhaps there are even fewer crooks. The following morning I was reminded of the Marseilles of old. When I came down in the hotel I saw a conspicuously English-looking man with a wife of similar looks. As I had lived in the colonies for over four years, it was easy to recognise him as an administrator in some African land. They had with them a pointer and a setter. Soon those dogs would be covered with ticks.

The station of Marseilles is becomingly cosmopolitan, what with boat trains, the Blue Train and the *Mistral*. The train for Toulouse was a homely affair waiting beside a modest platform, ignored by its betters. The dining-car attendant assured me he had no objection to my taking my dog into the dining-car. That was the sort of concession made only to friends. In the *Mistral* or the Blue Train it just couldn't happen. We were entering a different, more intimate world. The train pulled out at one o'clock, and for some time it was for me a journey which consisted of recalling a journey of eight years ago, though under different conditions. I had taken train and travelled part of the way on the same line when I left Pétain's France to get back to England in 1941—England at that time was on the other side of the Pyrénées. Nîmes, Montpellier and Béziers had their niches in the gallery of my past.

In the dining-car we sat with an old Frenchwoman of considerable distinction, and with the carriage and deportment that even the nanny of the best-behaved child would point to as an example. The fourth person at the table was a cattle merchant, his breast pocket bulging with at least a king's ransom. In my uninitiated mind I tend to believe that cattle merchants should be held partly responsible for the numberless hold-ups and robberies of which one reads with monotonous regularity in French papers. They carry vast sums of money about, because deals in cattle are made in cash. If one sees a cattle merchant one can be certain he is laden with money. Moreover, it is easy to spot a cattle merchant, for they rather look alike. They are loud, boisterous, their countenances are greasy, they drink and eat heavily. It seems as if the fond parents could select already at birth the child that would or wouldn't turn into a cattle merchant in time. The one at our table had certainly been selected long before he became a toddler.

Souillac: the Market Square

Souillac: the Market Square

"I bought," he said as a matter of introduction, "a bullock in the Nièvre. It wasn't bigger than that." He showed with his hand how high the bullock was. "But what a bullock. A beauty, a perfect beauty." He named the price, then asked the old lady to take an apéritif with him. The old lady said she never took an apéritif. He tried to press her, but she remained adamant. He had fat hairy hands, laughed and spoke nineteen to the dozen, mostly of his trade. He ate and drank with gusto. He told us he knew a cattle merchant who had lived till eighty-two. The old lady finished her meal quickly, bowed politely and left.

"She has class," he said, looking after her admiringly, "real class." He thought for a while. "She has class," he said. "I am willing to bet with you that woman has class." I didn't take on the bet. "If a woman has class she has class. One can't buy it in shops." He shook his head. "Class: that's what she has."

Bores fascinate me: my wife didn't suffer them. All she wanted was to go back to our compartment: I was caught and stayed on. The cattle merchant was a mine of information. He travelled about a lot, went from market to market; nevertheless, I didn't ask for his opinion on hotels in Souillac or, as a matter of fact, anywhere else. I haven't lived many years in France without acquiring the knowledge that cattle merchants, like commercial travellers, are interested in food alone. Comfort and sanitation have no say when they pick their hotels. Food is predominant, and towns and districts are judged by the food they provide. One eats well in Lyons, one eats well in Bordeaux, food is perhaps too heavy in the Périgord, cheap in the Haute Loire, in Brittany fish is good of course but the cooking usually *fade*, in Burgundy it is excellent though expensive. As I didn't want to admit that the time I spent in his

7

loquacious company was entirely wasted, I asked: "Do you know Souillac?"

"I do," he said.

"What is it like?" asked my wife.

"Foie gras and truffles. Will you have another bottle of wine?"

"No, thank you," I said. "We must go back to our compartment."

"Then I'll have to drink it alone. You will agree with me that there are worse occupations in the world."

"There are indeed," I said, and we parted.

In Toulouse the Tramontane was waiting for us. It brought the cold of the Pyrénées along with its own anger. The wide avenues and the wintry trees took its full impact. It is said of Toulouse in south-western France that it is a commercially minded town. Businessmen and commercial travellers consider that high praise. As I am neither, I found little to praise. Moreover, I have eaten better cassoulet elsewhere. I came back to Toulouse several times yet never succeeded in getting a truly good meal. On the other hand, prostitutes crowd the streets and bars. After dinner we wanted to walk along the tree-flanked avenues. The wind soon persuaded us to return to the hotel. In the morning we rose early in order to see the town before the train left for Souillac. Near the Hôtel du Midi, which is the best hotel of Toulouse, is a canal with a lock, a bridge follows. We didn't go farther: the wind was harsher than the night before.

"I don't like Toulouse," I said to my wife in the train. "The food isn't good."

"You begin to speak like a cattle merchant," she said.

II

From the train Montauban looked like a quiet, sleepy provincial town, a town whose inhabitants go early to bed,

and after nine in the evening only a few men remain abroad,
playing belotte silently in some lonely café. Such impressions
are unavoidably wrong. That year Montauban was to
distinguish itself with a vast case of concerted perversion in
which some dignitaries of the town were involved, school-
boys got into trouble and a suicide resulted. The station
was as sleepy as I imagined the town to be; then the train
left. It entered the land of rivers, poplars, tree-covered
mountains, bare mountains, the Causses, tunnels and
viaducts. We reached Cahors, and I didn't know that its
wine would become one of my favourite table wines. We
saw from the distance the Pont Valentré across which
had charged that great, alive man of the Midi, Henri IV.
Then we came to Gourdon, which was to play an, alas,
unhappy part in my life. Its fortified church stood on a
bleak hill above the town, the towers as if made ill-tempered
by the continuous wind. The next station was Souillac.

Notwithstanding occasional forebodings and presenti-
ments, one sails through life without knowing what to
morrow brings. That is a happy state, yet one often tries
to pretend one knew in advance. Little, therefore, would
be more pleasing than to be able to record, that as I alighted
from the train in Souillac, I knew and sensed that I had
arrived in a town which I would consider in a fashion an
ever-recurring home for the rest of my life. I had no such
presentiment.

The station of Souillac is at the end of a huge viaduct
which is almost a full circle. The station faces a deep valley
dominated by the viaduct. Behind the station are modern
houses of no attraction, and those houses accompany the
traveller till he reaches the town proper. With the oustalous still in mind, we weren't unduly optimistic as we
looked round. Admittedly it was warmer than it had been
the entire winter on the Riviera, but the houses, yes the

houses, were too near the knuckle. If I had obeyed my first impulse I should have got back into the train and gone elsewhere. We left the luggage, heard the whine of a saw mill, and walked towards the town.

It isn't easy to recapture the first impression when so many others follow, pushing the first one inch by inch into the background. We didn't notice the admirable church with its three cupolas before we were well in the town. Nowadays I can see it from the station, because I look out for it. But we heard a lion roar. I maintain the first sound of Souillac was the roar of a lion for me. It was half-past-twelve and the lion of a visiting circus was waiting for its meal. I was to hear in time to come the nightingales: but the roar of the lion came first.

We took the long high road instead of the short one that goes past the cemetery. The cemetery of Souillac, as is often the case in France, especially south of the Loire, has as important a position as, say, the grand café or the market place.

One accepts death south of the Loire in a healthy, re-signed manner, but one doesn't turn one's back on the dead. Mausoleums are built for them, flowers are brought to them and one goes to the cemetery simply to visit them. In Souillac I knew a man whose wife had died recently. He called on her every day. I often went by the cemetery and saw him standing beside her grave. A spring afternoon he came out as I was passing, and we walked away together.

"I usually go to see her," he said, "to tell her what's happening in the town. She loved gossip." He was silent for a while. "Besides, I don't see why she shouldn't know how business is and what the family is doing."

He was by no means a morbid man. In some village of the Lot, so I was told, a widow went to her husband's grave after a thunderstorm and upbraided him; for, she explained to him, he knew perfectly well that lightning frightened her. He up there in Heaven should have done something to prevent it.

As I have said, my wife and I took the long road, and the modern, ribbon-built houses and garages increased our fears. Luckily we lost our way, that is turned off by mistake to the right. Soon we found ourselves in the market place, and there our fears left us. We were in a small square, grey and ageless. Facing us was a chemist's shop with a genteel shop-window belonging to the end of the last century. That and the four pillars holding the roof of the market were the only comparatively recent features of the square. The market was empty, the townsfolk were at dinner, peace reigned, hardly a sound, the old stones, sprayed, alas, with cement, alone ruled; theirs, however, was an aloof rule. In the other square had stood the statue of Admiral de Verninhac, a native of Souillac who had brought over to France the Obélisque of Luxor. The Germans removed the statue, and after the war a mild desire flickered in some Souillagais breasts to offer the admiral a new statue. The left-wing mayor saw no point in doing so. Thus the admiral is without a statue: on the other hand the Obélisque remains in the Place de la Concorde, which the admiral probably would prefer.

We walked up to the Promenades past the belfry. The belfry is of the thirteenth century, partly demolished yet imposing; the church was burned by the Huguenots. Now and then it is asserted that the English were the culprits. The church, which is no longer a church, houses at the present time the fire brigade and the somewhat garish town hall, which twice a week is turned into a cinema. Next to it is the Grand Hôtel.

The Promenades are but a section of the Route Nationale,

that is of the Paris–Toulouse road. On one side are the notaire's office, the tobacconist, Banque Populaire, M. Sansfourche's garage, a pastry shop and the four leading cafés of Souillac. One of them, the Étoile, is purely political: needless to add, it is the Communist café. On the other side, or rather in the middle, is a newspaper kiosk, behind it three rows of clipped plane trees, and in their shade in summer the terrace of the Grand Hôtel.

"Let's have first a look at the Grand Hôtel," I said. We went in, and once again I was unaware that I would spend months on end year after year at the Grand Hôtel. But I was already impressed by Souillac's curious gift of space and freedom, a gift most French provincial towns knowingly lack.

A woman sat behind the desk in the office. She rose. She was like a charming and dignified Queen Victoria, her masses of brushed-up blonde hair her crown. Her sceptre was of wisdom and iron; and I have seldom found a better trained staff than that of the Grand Hôtel. She was Madame Couderc the wife of Monsieur Pierre Couderc, the proprietor. She became a good and true friend of my wife and myself. She died less than a year later, and in her Souillac lost more than it could ever find again.

We decided to stay at the Grand Hôtel: the decision came easily. We were given a room overlooking the Promenades and also the cinema. On Saturdays and Sundays we heard the films from our room. I recommend listening to the cinema without seeing what happens on the screen. It is a good exercise for the imagination. Who is kissing whom? Who says I love you? And why? What caused that eerie shriek? Is that clapping or a railway engine? Is it an aeroplane arriving or the rattle of a machine gun? In one film a male voice sang "Coming Round the Mountain" five times. I still wonder why.

After luncheon we went at once to find the Dordogne.
It is said of the Dordogne that it breaks loose from the
grasp of the mountains at Souillac. That is exaggerated.
True, it turns west after Cazoulès and for a while flows on
fairly liberated; it is soon gripped by the mountains again.
We reached the river beside a bent, tired signpost bearing
the legend Baignade. Near the signpost was a scrap-heap,
farther on broken bottles abounded. The river was rather
low. It was of perfect beauty, and when I say that I know
in all humility precisely what that implies. Behind us were
little houses and little plots which seemed in appearance
to have something in common with the scrap-heap; before
us, the slowly flowing water, the willows on the bank, the
poplars everywhere, the mountains running on each
side of the river, and upstream was the bridge built
at the beginning of the last century, pleasing and sober.
And among the willows patient men fished. They fished
with much conviction and small reward. The colour of the
Dordogne in winter is a mixture of grey and yellow with
sudden patches of blue. Near the bridge the houses come
down to the edge of the water. The port was near the
bridge: before the Dordogne was straddled by hydro-
electric dams, barges came from Bordeaux to Souillac.
Nowadays the popular craft on the river is the canoe of the
holiday-maker in summer. More appropriate and sympathetic is the ferry at Cieurac.

The Dordogne in the old days used to flood after the
long rains, which can be pretty savage in the Lot. At the
present time the dams keep the river within respectable
bounds. In the winter of 1950 it rained a good deal and the
river was high. It was a fine sight to watch the unsuspecting
river glorying in its man-allowed savagery. Branches and
other innocent things were rushed along, under the bridge
a whirlpool made fools of them for a while; at Cieurac the

ferry, owing to the speed of the river, crossed over in an amazingly short time—the ferry runs, as it were, along a wire rope at a certain height, held by a pylon on each bank— and all that glory ceased when it suited those who rule the dams.

It became our habit to walk along the river every day. The following winter when the river was high a little boy appeared from behind a half-submerged willow and trotted beside me.

"The water," he said, "is very high."

"Very high," I said, and hurried on because I didn't like his podgy face. He began to run at my side.

"Not far from here," he said, "just beyond Cazoulès, the corpse of an old lady was found among the willows."

"Yes," I said, and the rain beat down and I walked even faster. He was practically galloping beside me.

"Drowned," he said gleefully. "She was bloated too. Very bloated. In summer the water is much lower. One can wade across."

"Do you wade across?"

"I do," he shouted, because he couldn't keep up with me, "but only with my comrades. They look after me. I don't want to end up like the old lady."

A cautious little boy; and whenever I met him he grinned at me and gave me a look as if we shared some bloated secret.

That first afternoon, after we had gone as far as the ferry, we went to look at the cafés facing the Grand Hôtel. The Communist café was a forbidding-looking place. I soon found out that only the Communists frequent it. If anybody else goes there he is soon roped into an argument, preferably on doctrine. The argument is one-sided and intolerant. In fact, as a Souillagais of no strong political opinions put it to me, if one says in there it won't rain tomorrow one is immediately shouted down, attacked and treated as an idiot and a traitor. Even in Souillac life is too short for that sort of thing. Next to it was the Café de Paris. The Café de Paris is owned by Madame Sabatié, an elderly woman, born up on the plateau, the daughter of peasants, and of unshakable will-power. She had come down to Souillac at the beginning of the 1914–18 war, starting with a small shack in which she cooked for the many Russians who at that time were working in and around Souillac. They were a rough crew and her work was hard. The fruit of her work is the Café de Paris, the three-storey building which houses it, and a farm. Her grand-daughter married an official in the Ministry of Finance. Thus it goes.

That first afternoon I met the man whose presence in Souillac contributes a great deal to my recurring desire to visit Souillac. He is an Alsatian, his name is Pierre Betz, he edits that excellent publication called *Le Point*. It was through him that I came to know the town and its inhabitants. Without his help and knowledge most of this book would have remained unwritten, and consequently the rest wouldn't have been born either.

Betz came to Souillac, as many Alsatians came into south-western France, at the outbreak of the 1939–45 war when Alsace was evacuated. And in Souillac he remained. He is the secretary of the Syndicat d'Initiatives, and is of intelligent and erudite help to anybody who wants to know more of the district than the stereotyped leaflets for tourists vouchsafe. He became an intimate friend of my dog; for it was he who discovered that Jamie, my dog, had but one ambition in life, namely to become a horse. And Jamie would run a race with himself beside the Dordogne. He invariably won.

One can't move about France without knocking one's

elbow against bygone wars. The last two wars are especially at one's elbow. Here a father had been killed in the first, there a brother disappeared in the second, over there a family's fortune was made in one and lost in the other. The last two wars are responsible for migrations which aren't the privilege only of human beings. The forests which spread towards Cahors, and in every other direction too, are the abodes of wild boars. There aren't many to be found these days, but when wars break out the number of them increases. For as soon as firing starts in the great forests of the east, the wild boars leave and trot and grunt towards the forests of south-western France. That, one must admit, is an enchanting picture. The big guns of the Maginot Line open up, father *sanglier* gathers his kin round him and they start off for the quiet of the Lot. Their forbears had acted in the same manner when the field guns and rifles began to rattle twenty-five years earlier. Perhaps some of them, fancying a short cut, trotted through the dark streets of Lyons at night; and according to what I know of the early-to-bed habits of the Lyonnais, they probably went through the streets unchallenged. When wars come to an end they go back east, hence their present small number in the south-west. Some hermit, living alone in a forest, might at some future date look round and see that the number of wild boars has increased. "War again," he will say and thank God that he is a hermit.

Sunday shooting is as embedded in Souillac life as fishing in the river or playing poker. On Sunday mornings one sees small, ferocious groups getting ready for the day's sport. Two or three men with guns on their shoulders, their half-starved dogs barking enthusiastically beside them, go off to the nearest café to gather the necessary strength. A little later they are off, either on bicycles or in old cars. In the evening, provided they were lucky, they return with

one rabbit. There might be even a partridge, but that is as
rare as two rabbits. They often complain of their half-
starved dogs, because the dogs, when they either find the
shot rabbit or catch the running rabbit, simply take it to a
quiet spot and devour it. Nevertheless, the good sportsman
of Souillac stubbornly believes that an underfed dog is *par·
excellence* the ideal shooting dog.

I knew a Souillagais shot who went shooting in an un-
orthodox fashion; that is he ran over his rabbit. He explained it wasn't easy, because the wheel of the car, if
the car wasn't manœuvred cleverly, might easily make
pulp of the rabbit. He boasted of his prowess and once
showed me a rabbit which looked beautifully undamaged.

The great shooting days come towards the middle of
March, when the woodpigeons are on their way to the
northern countries. They come by the thousand and darken
the evening sky. My wife and I frequently walked out of
Souillac, and stood and watched them as they settled down
on the trees in the dusk. The trees on the mountainside
looked as if they were laden with heavy fruit. A shot rang
out and they rose, turning the sky into the colour of the
not distant night. Then the dusk would come into its own
again temporarily as they settled down on the trees. A
rivulet flowed in the valley, the trees near us were wrapping
themselves in darkness, in the distance the sound of a train
reverberated against the mountain; another shot, and now
we only felt them up in the air, because night had sailed
in. The *palombes*, that is, the wood pigeons, are esteemed
for another reason too. The husband takes his gun and
tells his wife he is off to shoot pigeons in the dusk; the
loving, anxious wife reminds him of countless lurking
dangers such as slipping on the mountainside in the dark,
and while she hopes he will come to no harm the husband,
unnoticed in the dusk, slips with a girl friend into a hotel,

or takes her down to the river bank. When he comes home he complains of his bad luck: his wife consoles him and says better luck next time.

The café next to the Café de Paris is the Café du Quercy, named after the district. Administratively Souillac is in the Department of the Lot, historically in the Quercy, which is part of Guyenne. Though both these cafés are patronised by what I should call Souillac Café Society, there is a subtle distinction between them. Some members of the Society go only to the Café de Paris, others only to the Quercy. There are several reasons: habit, old feuds, old quarrels; also at given moments one café is more popular than the other. Most members go to both of them; nevertheless, a subtle distinction remains. Generally speaking, the gamblers prefer the Café du Quercy because it is nearer to the Cercle. The manager of the Quercy, Monsieur Fernand, is a friend of mine. He hails from Montpellier, and his wife is from Brittany, but they belong by now so much to Souillac that if they left it wouldn't be the same place. Some towns can absorb individuals: some individuals, however, can absorb towns.

Poker is the leading card game. It is played noisily, angrily, played till dawn, no quarter is given, only expected. Friendships cease, avarice and avidity take their place and till the game is over they alone rule. The Souillagais, so one of them put it, is an excellent winner. The trouble is that to lose is considered to be foolish, and nobody in the town likes to think he might be a fool. Moreover, the virtuous should win; and everybody takes himself for a virtuous man, which makes gambling difficult. I witnessed unpleasant rows, heard insults flying, yet a few days later, if not the next day, the enemies of the night were friends again. I heard men swear a sacred oath they wouldn't play with so and so, ever, yes, ever. Three days later they were at the same table. After all, there isn't much else to do at night in Souillac.

One night we heard a small child howling in the room next to ours. It was nine o'clock, and to judge by the noise, the child had settled down to a night's bitter howling. I rang for the maid and asked her why the child shrieked and sobbed so lustily. Apparently the child's father was an inveterate and unlucky gambler. He had come to play at the Cercle that night. He had been rich, but most of his wealth was taken from him at poker. He couldn't afford any more servants, so when he went gambling he had to take the baby along.

"The child cries," said the maid, "because it knows papa will lose."

One of my Souillagais friends frankly confessed to me that he had won over a million francs shortly after the war.

The poker players are, needless to say, a small sect; rugby is the true game of Souillac. The townsfolk wait for Sunday to see Souillac win, and if Souillac loses then it is no Sunday. In the season I should recommend to those who are addicted to noise to go to the Quercy after Mass and listen to the day's team being selected; and for those who like to look at broken noses and bleeding knees the afternoon's game should be a welcome sight.

And here I can't but lament the inroad sport has made on the most civilised nation in the world. The idea of sport ought to be, I suppose, exercise, team spirit, fresh air, health and the like. The young men of France when not longing for a fifteen horse-power Citroën or, if more modest, for a four horse-power Renault, think of sport, speak of sport, read of sport. South of the Loire rugby is the game, the one and only, and I often had the feeling that if one opened the skull of any young man of Souillac, instead of finding the names of Richelieu, Berlioz and

Rimbaud, one would find a bleeding nose. The youths of the town stand fidgety and excited in front of the newspaper kiosk: in a few minutes the sports papers will arrive, and they stand and wait there every afternoon.

The young men of Souillac read no books. It isn't easy to blame them. If one reads, a certain amount of concentration and imagination is needed. Cinema, television and sports demolish both, and, which is worse, make them unnecessary. Why bother to visualise Tom Jones or Uncle Toby or Eugénie Grandet when the cinema gives one the complete works, television caters for a sedate, thoughtless evening at home, and rugby whips up cruelty, ambition and hero worship? Why admire Flaubert when there are fifteen members of the rugby team to be adulated.

I talked to several schoolmasters; one agreed with me, the others disagreed, because they too thought that one's function in life was either to play or to watch rugger.

III

The Quercy is the home of truffles: truffles are one of the mainstays of Souillac. On market days in winter men stand about furtively in the market square. Furtively because truffles shouldn't be sold privately. The price of truffles varies year by year; in fact, there can be huge differences in price. In 1949, for instance, the price of truffles was four hundred and fifty francs, in 1951 six thousand. During the cheap years always the same few men buy up the truffles and sell them in the years of high prices. The same few men; for nobody else thinks of doing the same, and when they make their vast packet of money everybody else bemoans his own luckless fate. "You will see," said my friend Betz, "that when truffles are cheap again exactly the same will happen." Which shows the gift of making money is simply a knack.

A village not far from Souillac owned a communal sow which sought out truffles. The sow took to eating truffles and the villagers didn't know at first what to do. A meeting was held and it was decided to buy a muzzle. The muzzled sow was taken out to look for truffles, but she showed no desire to do so. She strolled about, the oaks left her cold, her muzzled nose was in the air—in short there were no truffles. Another meeting was held and now it was decided to use cunning tactics. They took her out unmuzzled, the idea was that once she found the truffles she would be "shooed" off and the truffles picked. All went well for a while, but then to the consternation of the villagers no more truffles were found. For what happened was this: the wise sow took them to some tree where she knew no truffles dwelt, and once she was pushed away, she went to the tree where she knew she would have a good tuck in, and ate the truffles in peace.

For my personal taste and palate there are too many truffles served in too many dishes both in the Quercy and the Périgord. The word *truffé* loses its magic. It is an acquired taste, consequently it can be lost easily. Nonetheless, fortunes can be made on that acquired taste which in the long run tires the palate.

Tobacco growing is the other important industry of the district. It is grown on the plateau and in January the peasants cart down the tobacco to sell it to the state monopoly. The peasants of the Quercy are a dour lot who come to town but rarely, spend little and stick together like sheep. Their business done, they walk in groups; if one falls back he rushes after his companions as though afraid that were he left behind he would be lost for ever. They don't smile. They are dressed in black, wear black hats and take no notice of the townsfolk. If the leader of a group goes into a café the group follows him albeit the leader himself has chosen the café at random. The leaders, so a Souillagais pointed out, should wear bells round their necks. They don't stay for long. As the hour of the midday dinner approaches they get into the lorry which brought them down from the plateau, and drive home; for why spend money on food when there is the hard-worked wife at home preparing the midday meal?

One night a chemist of Souillac was wakened by somebody knocking loudly on his locked front door. The chemist was in bed, so he waited for the knocker to go away. But the knocks became frantic, so he rose and went to the window, and in the dark street stood a peasant. "What do you want?" shouted the chemist.

"Forgive me, monsieur," said the peasant, "but it is the cow. She is very ill. I can assure you, monsieur, I wouldn't have wakened you if it had been the wife. But it is the cow. Monsieur, the cow."

The peasants speak the language of Oc, French seldom and only when they are forced to. Money is sacred to them. When they come to sell their tobacco they receive vouchers which are paid a month or so later. The banks of Souillac put out notices saying they will discount the vouchers at one in a thousand. The peasants prefer to wait.

During the occupation the Gestapo was at Cahors. It came to Souillac now and again, took its victims and returned to Cahors. It was usually known in advance for whom the Gestapo would be looking. One day for escaped prisoners, another for Jews, and then rumour reached Souillac they were coming to take away the Alsatian refugees. An Alsatian living at the Grand Hôtel was warned in time and he took to the mountains. It was easy enough to disappear on the plateau, especially as the peasants never refused to shelter fugitives. The Alsatian arrived on a farm and asked the peasant for asylum. It was a house with two rooms, yet the peasant told him to sleep in the same room with his wife and himself; and the Alsatian witnessed for a whole year the peasant's matrimonial life in all its aspects. At the end of the year a young woman, also on the run, appeared and asked to be taken in. The peasant sent the Alsatian into the next room: it was the girl's turn to sleep with the couple. After the war, when the Alsatian had already left, the peasant explained to him that he kept his hoard of gold hidden in the next room, but by the time the girl appeared he had reached the conclusion that the Alsatian could be trusted. I met that peasant in Souillac and asked him whether the story was true.

"Yes, indeed," was the answer. "I could trust him completely. At times I even left him alone in the house for half an hour."

The peasant's life is hard. His house, which is often no better than a stable, is unheated in winter and lacks all comfort. But the peasant has no need for it: he works the entire day, comes in only for meals, in the evening eats in the kitchen and then, fully dressed almost, falls into bed. During my second visit to Souillac I was taken to see a farm. It was a warm evening. The peasant was elderly, had a squint and looked drunk. "But not with drink," said the man who had taken me. "Work."

The peasant's treat is market day. Markets are held twice a month in Souillac: on the fourth and nineteenth. Unfortunately for the lovers of simplicity, the markets have lost their romance: they are organised affairs, organised, as it were, by big business. The giant vans, filled with goods, go from market to market in the course of the week— they are in fact stores on wheels. Shoes, cloth, stockings, shirts, saucepans, underwear, hats and the rest of the bag of tricks could be bought just as well in the shops. The local tradespeople eye market day unfavourably. Yet for the peasant market day means a day of outing and shopping. Point out to him that a pair of *sabots* is cheaper in the shop, still the peasant will buy it at the stalls.

The life of those who cater for market day is equally un-romantic. They are—and that is the long and the short of it —travelling shopwalkers. They arrive in the morning in their vans, display their goods, stand about as shopwalkers do and pick their noses when not selling. In the evening they pack up, go off to Sarlat or Brive or Bergerac, and the same humdrum selling begins next day. The cafés profit from market day because the same ambulant shopwalkers eat in the same café every time they come.

On market days frequently arrive the publicity lorries of firms like Pernod and Ricard. They are covered wagons and usually a huge bottle is displayed on the roof. Inside the lorry is a gramophone, and the loudest of loudspeakers relays in a noisy, cracked voice advertising songs. ''I'll see you in my dreams, but only with a bottle of Ricard glued to your rosebud lips,'' or something to that effect,drowns all sound in the market. Those publicity monsters come back every two hours and leave only in the evening. No orders are solicited: the traveller will come in the wake of the publicity van in a week's time. Indeed, like so much else, market day is becoming more and more impersonal. The cattle and sheep market in the market square, near the church and also near the war memorial, is a different affair. There peasant buys from peasant. I often watched buying and selling; the animal is denigrated, found fault with, and when the deal is done the insulted beast is carried off in triumph. During the deal one laughs a certain amount. Sardonic laughter and angry laughter. After the deal nobody laughs any more.

The shopkeepers of Souillac are detached from the speed and rush which modern business life entails. If one goes to a shop and buys a dozen shirt buttons, the shop closes behind one and the shopkeeper goes off to fish. Of hurry and the urge for money little evidence is found. Souillac boasts of many shops, small shops, large shops, and they are most of the time innocent of customers. One can't help wondering how their owners earn a living. Almost every shop sells picture postcards; for Souillac proudly considers itself a tourist centre. Monsieur Lavergne, the president of the Syndicat d'Initiatives, and Betz, who is the secretary, work hard for the tourist trade; the others look on and sell picture postcards to the tourists.

Yet there was one exception which nearly caused a civil war. It was at any rate a minor Clochemerle, though there was nothing scabrous about it. The Syndicat d'Initiatives was housed near the garage facing the Grand Hôtel. For some reason or other the Syndicat couldn't stay in that building, and a new home had to be found. The plan was to build a small kiosk somewhere. With that the town unanimously agreed. Nobody agreed about the site. The logical thing would have been to put it up on the Promenades before the Grand Hôtel. The other hotels—not very good hotels— hotly objected. The kiosk in front of the Grand Hôtel would mean more trade for the Grand Hôtel. It was useless to argue that without the Grand Hôtel Souillac would have no tourist trade. The idea had to be dropped; and suddenly every tradesman in Souillac became tourist-conscious. Everyone offered a site before his shop, or next to the shop. The conclusion was reached to put the kiosk on the Route Nationale, since most tourists arrived by car and the Route Nationale is, while going through Souillac, the high street too.

"Did you hear that?" shouted to me an irate shopkeeper from the lower part of the town. "Did you? The Route Nationale? To suit the others? Who are we who have our shops elsewhere? Yes, who are we? Beasts? A class without rights? Was the Revolution for this? Were we liberated for this?"

Perhaps Napoleon retreated from Moscow for this, I said, but not aloud. Never were Lavergne and Betz more sought after men; and no solution was in sight. When I came back nine months later I came upon the perfect solution. The kiosk stands at the bifurcation of the road to Sarlat. One side faces the Route Nationale, the other the Sarlat road. There is asphalt round it, cars whisk past right and left, but there is no shop, no hotel and no café in the vicinity. Stuck in the middle of neutral asphalt it brought home once more to the Souillagais the meaning of liberty, equality and, I suppose, fraternity.

Politics play a vital role in Souillac, as they do in most provincial French towns. They are often a matter of personalities, little rivalries, small ambitions thwarted, and the fear of ridicule. One small episode which I witnessed should put them in their right and, in a sense, quite cosy perspective.

A conseiller général had to be elected, and the position of a conseiller général is enviable and much sought after. One of the middle-of-the-way parties, that is a party whose members are violently anti-clerical once they have made sure that their wives pray for them regularly in church, had its candidate, so had other parties, and when the election approached, the middle-of-the-way candidate stood aside for a slightly-left-of-the-way candidate because he didn't want to split the anti-Communist vote. That was a praiseworthy and fruitful gesture, and nobody deserved more the ribbon of the Légion d'Honneur than the self-sacrificing middle-of-the-way candidate. He received the ribbon and his party decided to give a sumptuous dinner in his honour. The ex-candidate invited a cabinet minister from Paris for the dinner, and the plan was for the cabinet minister to decorate him in the course of the banquet. The new chevalier was on bad terms with the Préfet, and for that good reason didn't invite him. Unfortunately, the minister was busy with an impending vote of confidence and wrote to say he couldn't come. Who, was now the urgent question, should give the ex-candidate his order? The Préfet was out of the question, so the Sous-Préfet was approached. He, however, pointed out that if the Préfet wasn't coming he couldn't attend either. Thus the banquet had to be abandoned.

"We are," said the local chairman of the party, "the laughing stock of the whole world. I bet we will read about it tomorrow in *Pravda*."

Souillac laughed for a few days. Those who laughed loudest were his own party members and private friends. Then it was all forgotten, because Sunday came and the rugger team had to be selected, which was more important.

Politics, it is said, are deeply engraved in the hearts of schoolmasters. In Souillac I became friendly with three, and only one was interested in party affairs. He was a Socialist and defended Socialism as one defends a lost cause. The other schoolmasters preferred to exercise their talents at poker. The Socialist schoolmaster wanted to become the mayor: at the last elections the man who sells soda water and fruit juice was the one who got in.

There is in Souillac an agricultural college called Collège Technique. The peasants send their sons to the college because now that they must use tractors the sons should learn how to repair them. Thus, instead of it going to some garage, the repair money would stay in the family. Probably the sons will become mechanics, turning their backs on the farms of their fathers, and the garage keepers will continue to reap their reward. The pupils of the college are the young men who sit in the afternoons on the wall near the newspaper kiosk and wait for the sports papers. They excel too in foul language and aren't popular with the members of the Café Society.

The members of the Café Society might be called the élite of the town—at least they believe that. They play *belotte* in the evenings at the Quercy, on Sunday mornings they take their wives to the Café de Paris and the Quercy and stand them their Sunday apéritifs. During the week their wives stay at home. They are the well-to-do males of Souillac. They go to Brive and Toulouse; rarely to Paris, but when they go they lose their poise and hang about rather lost and frightened in the vicinity of the Gare d'Austerlitz. Their glamour melts.

The butchers rank high among the élite. Their number is legion, their fortunes increase daily and they bemoan their exalted position both in cafés and the Cercle. Apparently beasts should be much cheaper and meat more expensive. One of the butchers has a son who turned his back on the abattoir and became a hairdresser. The result is that he plays a less generous game of poker than the butchers. The saddler also plays poker and has luck. He plays, moreover, practical jokes. The hairdresser is his daily victim. The saddler now and then takes a pair of scissors and cuts off the hairdresser's tie; at other times he comes up from behind and the hairdresser finds his head inside a dark sack. The hairdresser's anger further encourages the saddler. I complimented the saddler on his deftness and sense of humour. Said the saddler: "I am far too witty for Souillac but not witty enough for Paris."

Then there is the stupidest man in Souillac, tall, pompous and grey-haired, who reels off old chestnuts; but such men can be found anywhere. Then there are many men and women who never go near the cafés. "But how do

The Abbey Church at Souillac

" Faire Chabrol "

they spend their time?" asked a leading member of the Café Society.

The local drunk spends his time and money with ease. He is a conspicuous figure because there is little drunkenness in Souillac. The representative of an insurance company got drunk one evening there. The population was horrified. It was even more horrified when it leaked out that the representative had tried in the course of his intoxication to rape the maid at his hotel. He tried it in the morning, which was inexcusable. A round robin was sent to the insurance company and the ill-fated fellow lost his job. Now the local drunk holds the fort of alcohol alone. I succeeded during the course of my several visits in piecing his daily life together, and in following him one can see a day of sorts in Souillac.

He frequently has difficulty in finding lodgings, as hotel and lodging-house keepers aren't partial to the habits he develops when under the influence of drink. Still, he manages to find a new roof every time he is asked to leave, and if he didn't he certainly wouldn't mind if he had to sleep in the open. He wouldn't notice the rain at night, and in summer it is cooler out of doors. He rises early, goes to a small café where he drinks a bottle of white wine. A few workmen of the saw mill and the conserve factory keep him company while they drink their coffee. He chats with them, for he is a man of erudition and at that fresh hour he is master of his thoughts and memories, though, as he confessed to me, he drinks because he wants to be rid of them. With the bottle of white wine begins his regular search for oblivion. The workmen go off when the discreet siren of one of the factories announces it is eight o'clock. The drunk leaves with them and walks along the Route Nationale. He walks carefully, and if he hears or sees a car he gets out of its way. He goes to another café which is in the lower part of the town. There he drinks more wine, then towards ten o'clock he changes over to apéritifs. The life of the town pulses round him, he idly watches a butcher carrying a carcase, the newspaper vendor pushing his bicycle, an old woman taking vegetables to the market. He watches them benignly and has another drink. When he leaves the café he treads less carefully but still looks out for vehicles. He goes to a third café, where he reads the morning papers. He reads leisurely, every bit of news is scrutinised, and then he reads the papers again. The siren above the Mairie goes at twelve, Sundays excepted. At twelve he puts down the papers, pays for his drinks and goes to eat his midday meal.

"I studied English at school," he told me one day on his way to his lodgings, "and I know that the letter h doesn't exist in English. A curious language."

He eats little but drinks a lot with his meal. After luncheon he walks to the station, but doesn't walk straight any more. He drops his stick at intervals and his attitude to cars is somewhat haughty. If they won't get out of his way they will have to suffer. At the station he drinks heavily in the buvette. The dignity of the morning is discarded and the railway workmen laugh at him. Yet he has a new dignity of sorts, which consists of the greatness of achievement; for thoughts and memories have been dropped into the many glasses he has emptied. He drinks in the buvette till the Paris Express arrives. He waits for it, looks at the clock to verify whether the express is punctual. For nothing on earth will he leave the station before the express goes. Once the express has left he leaves the buvette. He walks back to the town, moving in the middle of the road, taking no notice of cars and lorries. The bigger the car the less he cares. The conquest of his better self is complete. He then drinks in several cafés and sees the men he saw in the morning now returning from work. He doesn't recognise them. Towards evening he starts for his lodgings—a painfully progressing, happy man. The practical jokers of the town often waste their time by driving up in their cars from behind, hooting noisily, the radiators of their motors hardly an inch from his back: but oblivious of them he quietly saunters on. He reaches his lodgings and falls into bed. In the morning thoughts, memories and drink wait for him.

Next to those already mentioned, dogs play an integral part in the life of Souillac. There are many dogs, most of them rarely fed. They roam the streets, beg on the hotel terrace, lie in the sun on the Route Nationale, get in the way of cars, eat out of dustbins, and when a bitch is on heat they gather on the Promenades. Some come from the plateau, some travel from distant villages. They stay for days, the small ones stay as long as the large ones, notwithstanding that the largest of them has already been chosen by the bitch. They follow the loving couple from street to street, fight among themselves, especially the hopeless small ones at the end of the queue. The bridegroom turns back, growls at them, they shrink away, then come back. At intervals the small ones detach themselves from the queue and all take part in a perverted romp; then they close in again. The bridegroom is mostly a butcher's dog; for butcher's dogs are well fed, consequently up to the exacting task. When the honeymoon is over the dogs disperse, only to return for the next betrothal.

Fishing in the Dordogne binds poor and rich together. Nearly everybody fishes, fishes for hours, and little is caught. There is much talk of secret pools in the tributaries of the Dordogne. But that is more a matter of secrets than of catching fish. On the other hand, I frequently ate perch and pike at the Grand Hôtel.

The food of the Quercy is heavy, and the heavier the more it is esteemed. One eats on every possible occasion. My friends often drove me around four in the afternoon to some not too distant inn where we drank wine, ate sausages, fumed ham, radishes and lashings of bread and butter. That is called faire les quatre heures. The four p.m. can last till seven p.m., then back to Souillac and dinner.

It isn't only in the afternoon that the Souillagais appetite is strong. The morning will do just as well; and one early morning I had to go to Gourdon. A bus leaves Souillac at a quarter to seven and reaches Gourdon at nine, which means it takes over two hours to cover twenty miles. The evening before my departure I was counselled to study the habits of the driver.

It was a cold spring morning, spruce and as if scrubbed with a brush. The sky was blue and high, every tree and every stone seemed to be on its own; and the still invisible sun was approaching the plateau. I stood waiting outside the Grand Hôtel. The town was awakening: the newspaper vendor arrived and unlocked the door of the kiosk, the P.T.T. service van stopped outside the post office and the Communist café's shutters went up; the other cafés remained asleep. A few people crossed the square, eyes red with sleep, faces hardly washed. The bus came, the newspaper vendor took his parcel of morning papers, I got in, the sole passenger, and the bus moved off. It was like travelling in an aeroplane, so noisy was the engine. The air was bitterly cold.

The Dordogne in the morning light looked as unfriendly as a pretty débutante who doesn't smile. Our first stop was Lanzac on the other side of the bridge. It is a pleasing village; but most villages please the eye in the Lot. No house in the village had any form of sanitation, but it is the same in most villages. The driver got out to deliver the mail and stayed away for a considerable time. That roused my suspicions, and when he climbed down from his seat in the next village I followed him. We went into a decrepit house. The room was smoky, the ceiling low. It was the inn and the post office too. A wood fire burned in the small fireplace, the smoke blowing straight into the room, which smelt of generations of unwashed humanity. An old man was pulling his trousers on, an old woman stood next to him, her apron filthy, a young woman sat with a baby in her arms, the baby squealed, and two filthy children were still asleep in a bed in the corner. In that bed their mother and the baby had slept with them a little while ago. On the table was a glass of marc—marc distilled at home; that glass was waiting for the driver. I asked for marc too. It burned its way into my fast of the night. Not an unpleasant sensation. The driver ate bread with his marc. As I left I nearly fell over a hen.

Our next halt was in a larger village with a regular post office. In the window of the house adjoining the post office appeared the stately head of an old man who in Cheltenham would immediately have been classed as a retired colonel. He stared hard at the bus, the driver, and the parcels the driver delivered. Then his head disappeared. The driver told me the old man was at the window every morning, and once the bus had arrived he wasn't seen at the window for the rest of the day. From the post office we moved on to the bistro. We had a drink, the driver didn't pay for his, which was natural enough since he took messages and parcels from village to village, was in fact the link with the world beyond the villages he visited. In the following village the driver had coffee with rum and half a loaf of bread.

At eight-fifteen we reached another village and by then we had a passenger. That passenger, because he hadn't studied the driver's habits carefully enough, stayed half an hour in the bus at Saint-Projet while the driver and I had breakfast. The local inn was half a grocer's shop and half a kitchen. We sat in the kitchen: the ceiling was low and two beds were in the corner. We were served with soup, greasy soup, and the driver poured red wine into it, lifted the plate to his mouth and drank the mixture of grease, fat, water and harsh, cold wine. That ceremony is called *faire chabrol*. Because I wanted to show off I followed suit. Half of the liquid stuff poured down my chin. Greasy sausages were fried on the kitchen range. The driver took two, and I, ready to go the whole hog, also took two. The home-baked bread was sour. The meal was, to say the least, remarkable. Conversation flowed: it was chiefly about the impending war. Curiously enough, in such off-the-map places, places that have the least to dread in case of war, the dread of war is rampant. Whether they believe or don't believe in the imminence of war depends on the last visitor's forecast. To that inn had come a lurid commercial traveller a fortnight before me. He had said there would be war in the summer. Now they were convinced that war was in the offing. I voiced the opinion that no war would come that summer. They cheered up and probably remained cheerful till the next man turned up from the outside world.

I was offered more soup and wine. I could have pushed my plate aside and said truthfully it wasn't for me. However, I drank as if my future depended on drinking that soup; as if all my friends were hoping that I wouldn't let them down by not drinking it; as if my enemies would rejoice if I left it; as if the prospects and happiness of my son depended on my drinking that soup. I was afterwards complimented by the three old women who had watched me drink, and by the driver too. They declared they wouldn't have believed that a foreigner could drink that soup—faire chabrol—and eat those sausages. I couldn't stick it a second longer. I smiled modestly, it was a sickly smile, and with perspiration streaming down my ice-cold forehead I hurried out. In the bus sat the passenger fretting. I envied him.

I saw the driver later on in Gourdon. It wasn't yet eleven o'clock. He was in a café eating bread and ham.

On trips like the one to Gourdon I couldn't help observing how badly the population of rural France is housed. Few people mind, which is food for thought, because nobody is more attached to his little comforts than the average Frenchman. And to boot, the Frenchman is a pampered person if compared to the Englishman who leaves his home to go to school, and once life begins for him in earnest he must make or find a home away from his parents. But the Frenchman lives with his mother; she spoils him; then he leaves his mother to be pampered and spoiled by a wife. In frequent cases mother and wife unite in keeping rain and wind away from him. They spend sleepless nights thinking up the dishes which might please him. A French friend of mine put it forcibly: "My only years of liberty," he said, "were the years of my military service."

Nonetheless, the comfort of the home means little to him. To sleep in a room which is no better than a stable somehow doesn't disturb his conception of comfort. The bathroom is negligible and the very idea of it is frequently overlooked. Here is a case in point. A man owned a shop, sold it, and had more money than he had ever possessed. He decided to spend part of his money on his house, which, like almost every house in Souillac, had no bathroom. He had, he told me, wonderful plans; I came back a year later and was asked round for a drink. The improvements consisted of a brand new dining-room suite straight from Levithan in execrable taste, and a radiogram. Needless to say, no bathroom had been added. On the other hand, it would be quite untrue if I said either he or the huge majority of his fellow citizens were less clean than a corresponding majority in an English market town.

If one speaks of housing they shed tears over their uncomfortable homes but add: "For us the table comes first." It undoubtedly does.

"Madame," said the wife of a local burgher to my wife, "you in England have no idea how we suffered here during the war. Take my husband and myself. We had a little hut up in the mountain and would repair with our friends to the little hut on Sundays. I would roast our midday meal on a spit. A chicken. A truffle. A thigh. A truffle. A wing. A truffle. Very big truffles. My speciality, madame. Now would you believe it? One Sunday we arrived at the little hut and the table was gone. Madame, that terrible Maquis had stolen our table."

The Maquis wasn't loved by all and sundry. Souillac was in the Maquis country and now and then the Germans came to Souillac. So did the maquisards, for it was boring at times up there in the Maquis. And the great fear of publicans and shopkeepers was that the Germans might run into them, in which case Souillac could share the fate of Oradour and Saint-Julien-Lampon. To be burned alive in a church with one's children wouldn't have helped the cause of France.

Moreover, it is ill-becoming for those who lived in a free fighting country like England during the war, to pass judgment on another country that was occupied, torn by strife, and where a knock on the door didn't mean the air raid warden coming round to say a light was showing.

Roc-Amadour

Turenne

Roc-Amadour

IV

My wife and I used to go for long walks, visiting the neighbouring villages of Lanzac, Pinsac and Cazoulès. In the beginning Pierre Betz, treating us as tourists expect to be treated, suggested we should climb the hill above the town and take a look at the tomb of the Gallic soldier—provided he was a Gaul and a soldier at that. Though I pressed for an answer nobody could explain why it was supposed that a Gaul was buried under that stone. "You must admit," said the saddler to me during one of his free moments—free from thinking up or playing practical jokes on the hairdresser—"that it sounds very fine. The tomb of the Gaul." The view from the tomb, however, was fine: Souillac a grey expanse with the belfry and three cupolas, the river turning in a half circle, on the right the viaduct almost a complete circle, a train outlined against the barren side of the mountain above Cazoulès, the château of Cieurac, the poplars ready to dance to lutes and flutes, and then not far from us I noticed a lonely railway line going off towards the mountains in a south-easterly direction.

"I wonder where that goes," I said.

"To Aurillac," said my wife, who took more trouble over facts than I.

"But that is in Auvergne," I said.

"The Haute Auvergne," she said, but she was never to see it.

A friend one day took us to the famous caves of Lascaux, which left me perplexed. We were taken round by a guide who pointed at a bull and said: "That was painted thirty-five thousand years ago." Then he pointed at another bull and said: "That was painted twenty-five thousand years ago." I couldn't help putting to myself the question: what happened in that studio in the intervening years? And another question I couldn't help asking either: where did those technically excellent painters study? For one can't paint 'like that without study and hard work. Whoever painted on the walls of Lascaux were great painters who knew uncannily well how to take advantage even of the curves of the caves. Could a civilisation have existed in the Neolithic age which only produced painting, and that of a very high standard? I read everything I could lay my hands on concerning Lascaux, and was even more puzzled. I would recommend Fernand Windel's *Lascaux* to those who put the same questions. It should be added that, surprisingly enough, no excavations have been carried out near the cave, though they might give the answers.

We took the bus to Sarlat, a town of Renaissance houses, but the good people of Sarlat are fed up with their Renaissance houses because the entire centre of the town is under the protection of the Ministère des Beaux Arts and no house can be repaired without the Ministry's permission, and no permit is granted for improvements inside the houses.

In Sarlat we found an agreeable hotel where the prices were lower than in Souillac. I said to my wife it might be a good idea to leave Souillac and spend some time and less money at that hotel. Before we made up our minds we strolled round the town, not so much looking at the house in which La Boëtie was born as at the very life of the town. Though it was market day the town was deadly. A cinema, a few sad cafés, and the surrounding country was of little interest either. Towards six o'clock a hush fell on the town, the hush of the approaching endless night. Even the way the inhabitants walked in the streets, the way they drank in cafés, was proof of the despondency of the town. There are many such towns in France; consequently it is hazardous to look at the map and decide suddenly to go to

such and such a town. The town should first be recon-
noitred; otherwise boredom might kill.

The point about Souillac is that one needn't fear boredom. It is an airy town hitched to the Route Nationale,
without the fear of loneliness, and one feels free in the
narrow, sunless streets seldom visited by the tourist; for
one can hear the train which is willing to take one to Paris
in seven hours.

In one of those narrow streets of Souillac, in the company
of other decrepit buildings, stands a house, and on the wall
is the bas relief of a scallop: the sign of St. James of Compostella. That house was for centuries the pilgrims' rest-
house. Through Souillac went the pilgrims to St. James,
and through Souillac they went too to Our Lady of Roc-
Amadour. The pilgrims are responsible in a sense for the
existence of Souillac: between April and September the
Dordogne could be crossed on foot near the old port which
is next to the bridge. (One always enjoys such simple and
logical explanations.)

Near the pilgrims' rest-house starts a narrow street,
lightless and smelly. It leads to a cheap café. On the outside
wall of that café a rusty chimney rises towards the almost
hidden sky. The chimney reminds one of the funnels of the
early steamships.

On top of the belfry the siren goes at noon. It would be
difficult to think of Souillac without the siren's noise; for
the siren is as much a native speciality as truffles. The
cracked bell of the belfry chimes twelve, the dogs of the
town come to the Promenades and howl with the siren.
They come from every direction. At eleven in the morning,
though the bell with its flat tin-like sound is rung eleven
times, no dog appears, but at twelve they come at the first
stroke as if they know that twelve follows eleven. The dogs
are led and marshalled by the Communist dog which leaves

the Communist café a few minutes earlier. Some of them test their voices: little whines, short howls, and much excited wagging of tails. Then the siren goes and they howl with gusto and conviction. When the siren stops the Communist dog shakes its ears and goes back to the café; the other dogs disperse and return next noon punctually. About a dozen dogs, including one with a limp, race daily to the square in order to partake of the cacophonic orgy.

My dog Jamie had lived in London most of the war, remaining till the end aloof from sirens. In Souillac, however, he didn't want to be left out: but he misunderstood the basic idea and instead of howling with the dogs he barked at them.

It was I who pointed out those siren concerts to my Souillagais friends. That wasn't surprising; for it is the duty of the stranger to whet the appetite of the native. Funny, they said, but Betz had also noticed them.

The howling of siren and dogs is a daily occurrence; another daily occurrence in which considerably more interest is evinced is, frankly, sex. It is discussed without any romantic trappings; in the evenings, especially during long, discreet winter evenings, it is practised in hotel rooms and beside the river. Love knows no barriers; and one of my friends walked into a hotel on a dark night. Nobody was about: he took his girl friend to a room: they stayed for two hours: they came down and still nobody was about. So they left. Incidentally, he was a friend of the hotel proprietor.

"Did you tell him when you saw him the next time?" I asked.

"No," he said, "by then it was too late and he would have been angry."

The approach to and practice of sex is simple, healthy; and D. H. Lawrence could never have become a popular writer among the Souillagais. I was told of a substantial citizen of the neighbourhood who would hear Mass with his wife every Sunday morning. He was respected and known for his decorum. After Mass he took her to a café and, as the French have it, installed her on the terrace. When he had made her comfortable and had ordered her drink, he left her to the weekly glass of vermouth. He crossed the road, and went into a shop, the door of which had been left open for him. A few seconds later the curtains were drawn in the windows above the shop. Behind those windows was the flat of his mistress. A little later he emerged through the shop door, crossed back to the café and sat down beside his wife, lifted his glass and, I suppose, drank her health.

The girls of Souillac at times desert their town. They go mostly to Paris, where they take on any old job, because in Paris they consider themselves superior to the other girls they have left behind. The expatriates come back now and then to show off and to visit relatives. They are caparisoned for the occasion, red finger and toe nails are caught by the sun and the envious eyes of the girls who stayed behind. It is also a sign of the changing sense of values that young peasants have a fair amount of difficulty in finding wives in the town. The girls prefer, for example, the drudgery of the post office to the hard, healthy and lonely life on the farms.

The desire to visit Auvergne took hold of me again in the middle of March 1949. The Souillagais were against it. Auvergne was the home of savages, boors, snow and rain. We should, if we insisted on going, go to Auvergne at some other time. The roads were snowed up.

"But I haven't a car," I said.

"That doesn't matter. You'd be snowed up even without a car."

"It is a very savage country," said somebody else.

"Do you know it?" I asked. It would have been a change to speak to somebody who knew Auvergne.

"Not exactly," was the answer, "but I come from the Corrèze, in fact from a village a few miles from the Cantal. Only a few miles, yet we in the Corrèze speak a different dialect. A few miles—but it is a case of two different continents."

The notaire was of the same opinion, and in a small town like Souillac one can't disregard the words of the notaire. The notaire is a man of influence and power: houses are bought and sold through him, wills, business deals, marriage contracts, in brief everything that smacks of money is within his province. In the temporal field the notaire has the same position as the curé in spiritual matters. The notaire must be friendly yet aloof; and the notaire explained to me that he invariably attended to deals of importance before meals. It is the custom to celebrate large deals with heavy food and much wine. "You see," said the notaire, "there is such a thing as good wine and bad wine. Those who drink the good wine are satisfied with the deal and become gay; but those who drink the bad wine regret the deal bitterly and say so. Therefore it is preferable to get the necessary signatures before wine is drunk."

"And Auvergne?" I asked.

"This time of the year I should go west and not east."

We decided to go west, and the day came to say goodbye for the first time to Souillac. I promised to return, but usually even the person who makes such promises disbelieves in them entirely. I was no exception. Yet as the bus which was taking us to Sarlat bumped past Cazoulès, I knew for certain that I would go to Souillac again. But not every traveller was so enthusiastic about the town of the church with three cupolas. Arthur Young, that serious

agriculturist of the late eighteenth century, had visited
Souillac in 1787. The day was June the ninth.

"Enter a different country," he wrote, "with the new
province of Quercy, which is part of Guienne; not near so
beautiful as Limousin, but to make amends, it is far better
cultivated. Thanks to maize, which does wonders! Pass
Noailles, on the summit of a high hill, the château of the
Marshal Duke of that name. Enter a calcareous country,
and loose chestnuts at the same time.

"In going down to Souillac there is a prospect that must
universally please; it is a bird's-eye view of a delicious little
valley, sunk deep amongst some very bold hills that enclose
it; a margin of wild mountains contrasts the extreme
beauty of the level surface below, a scene of cultivation
scattered with fine walnut trees; nothing can apparently
exceed the exuberant fertility of this spot.

"Souillac is a little town in a thriving state, having some
rich merchants. They receive staves from the mountains of
Auvergne by their river Dordogne, which is navigable eight
months in the year; these they export to Bordeaux and
Libourne; also wine, corn and cattle, and import salt in
great quantities. It is not in the power of an English
imagination to figure the animals that waited upon us here
at the *Chapeau Rouge*. Some things that called themselves by
the courtesy of Souillac women, but in reality walking
dung-hills. But a neatly dressed clean waiting-girl at an inn
will be looked for in vain in France."

He was, however, satisfied with the ferry, which he found
well contrived for driving in at one end and out at the
other "without the abominable operation common in
England of beating horses till they leap into them." The
fare pleased him too. Past Payrac he was shocked by the
number of beggars, and bemoaned that country women
and girls were without shoes or stockings, the ploughmen

43

without sabots. He was reminded of the misery of Ireland.

Arthur Young is the only English traveller whose name is known in Souillac. Whether anybody has read him is another matter. The picture of walking dung-hills might even irritate some of the women of Souillac, especially since at long last the town owns a shower-bath. It is interesting to note that the Dordogne was navigable for eight months. The exuberant fertility should be somewhat discounted. The drought can be so severe in summer that the peasants come down from the plateau to pick the leaves of the trees near the river to feed their cattle with them. Young was there in June, that is before the drought becomes serious.

Young was an enviable traveller who knew what he was looking for: agriculture; and history, architecture, habits and customs left him unmoved—in fact, they weren't much noticed. Before he came to Souillac he was impressed by the King of France's stud at Pompadour: horses; but the name Pompadour had no other meaning for him.

When I leave a town a hotch-potch of a canvas stays in my mind: the people I met, little episodes, a funny remark, and the squinting man I saw accidentally at a street corner. Trifles can light up the canvas with poignant clarity, even if they are silly and have little meaning. The day we left Souillac I bought from my friend the hairdresser a tube of shaving cream. It smelt, he said, of cucumber. I wasn't strong enough to resist the thought of cucumber, so I bought the tube and used it the same day. I don't think that cheeks tasting of cucumber would be a maiden's dream, but whenever I smell cucumber and wherever I smell it, I see the Dordogne, the church, the Promenades and can hear the dogs howling with the siren.

The bus was crowded because it was market day at

Sarlat. When I used to live in East Suffolk and drove around in order to explore East Anglia, I inevitably arrived at the town I wished to visit on early closing day, and thus savoured the deadly quiet of the streets. In France, on the other hand, I generally find myself squashed in buses because it is market day at my destination. The road followed the river. The March landscape appeared to be waiting for spring, waiting, however, with little conviction. The trees were as barren as the rocks on the edge of the water. We reached the sad village of Saint-Julien-Lampon. During the German occupation two young members of the Maquis came to Saint-Julien, and as it was warm bathed in the river. They left their arms in a house on the shore. The Germans found those arms, cordoned off the village, the inhabitants, men, women and children, were driven into the Church; the Germans then set it on fire. The villagers all perished in flames, and now, many years later, one still feels the tearful sadness of undeserved death and of unfulfilled lives. Beside the bridge is a memorial tablet, with the list of the dead, the names of the children—their Christian names alone—under the names of their parents. One cannot but feel anger and sorrow.

To speak of more cheerful matters, I went one day to Saint-Julien with two friends and we decided to remain for luncheon. On the other side of the bridge is a good restaurant, but it was closed that day. A bit farther on was a decrepit inn, and we decided to eat there. We ate in the garden, and as it had rained the night before our feet either dangled above or were in a pool of water. We were surrounded by not very silent watchers, mostly dogs and hens. The dogs fought each other, the hens pecked at our wet ankles, the food was bad, and the fitting climax came with the bill. It was three times as expensive as it would have been in the comfort and plenty of the Grand Hôtel.

I was so surprised that I paid without a murmur. The moral of the story is this: beware, traveller, of small mean inns: they are more likely to rook you than the expensive-looking restaurants.

The bus in which my wife, my dog and I were sitting stopped beside the bridge and the memorial tablet. The village was uncannily quiet, a cemetery pretending to be something else. A woman alighted, another woman got in, and those two women were the only two living souls I saw moving along the empty village street.

We left the bus at Sarlat, where we waited for the little off-the-record train to take us to Beynac. We walked the streets, and admired the house in which Étienne de la Boëtie was born in 1530. We went into that superb Renaissance house, but the smell of latrines was too strong. I couldn't help putting to myself that often-recurring yet unanswerable question: would the pleasure such fine old stones give to the eye be sufficient to induce one to dwell behind them? Or to put it differently: is the aesthetic delight enough? Yes is the instinctive answer, but don't the modern amenities near those stones make the yes somewhat insincere? Take away from Sarlat its few modern pleasures, leave it, as it could so easily be left, without them, move into Boëtie's house for good, and then try to answer. I believe that the approach of most of us to old towns and old houses is sentimental, aesthetic, historic, and they are no more and no less than open-air museums for us.

Straight from that house we went to the station and in the buvette a workman got into conversation with us. He pulled the talk towards himself in order to air the doctrines he had been carefully taught. He spoke of liberty, which should be curtailed because it might harm one's neighbour. I knew that line of argument, and thought it would be preferable to slide back into the sixteenth century. But would it? The rain had ceased, it was a little warmer and the man said history had proved everything he said.

In the little train we were back in time, though only taken to the middle of the last century—and even that is an exaggeration. But it must be admitted that the French Railways still keep in use on side lines remarkably old coaches. With us in the coach, which was a mixture of drawing-room, waiting-room and old-fashioned public lavatory, sat a soft, fat, intelligent Frenchman. He asked us where we were going. We said Beynac. He said it was too early in the season; then he said: "I wish I were English."

"Why?" asked my wife.

He explained, and his explanation was a further proof of a theory I have already spoken of in this book. According to him the middle-class, comparatively well-to-do Frenchman was coddled from the cradle to the grave. The mother coddled him till the wife took over, and now and then both women coddled him together. Here and there an unmarried sister or sister-in-law gave a helping hand. "I was in England with the Free French," he said. "Alone, madame." He beamed at us.

Though many Frenchmen of his class take mistresses, they fare no better with them; for the mistress wants to coddle him too. She considers herself a slightly inferior wife, but a wife all the same. Her ambition is to make him feel at home with her, as much at home as in his own house. Take a Frenchman, our travelling companion explained, who, for so it was arranged by the respective parents, marries into a large grocer's shop. He spends his day in the shop beside his wife and before he goes off to his mistress in the evening he discusses with his wife the rising price of

Camembert. He takes paper and pencil and figures out for her how high the new retail price should be. He meets his mistress in a café. She, in search of security and dignity, has succeeded in getting him to buy a flower shop for her. He sits down in the café, then asks her how things are with her and the shop. She is worried because the price of carnations is steadily rising. He suggests buying them in the South of France. She asks: what about transport? He asks for paper, takes a pencil from his pocket and figures out prices. Roses come after carnations, and they are both exhausted by the time they have finished. It is getting on, the grocer's shop will open early in the morning, so he leaves her, goes home and falls tired, his brain crammed with flowers and cheese, into bed beside his sleeping wife.

"Believe me," said the soft, fat Frenchman, "what with *les affaires* and being involved with two businesses, he gets little fun either from wife or mistress. Eventually comes a third woman if he is rich enough. She then gets a hat shop, and it starts all over again."

"Here we are," I said.

"Beynac," he said and put a scarf round his neck, buttoned his overcoat over it, but it wasn't cosy and warm enough like that, so he took another scarf from his suitcase, fumbled with it, but couldn't be bothered to tie it round his neck. He put it back into the suitcase and sighed.

"He misses them," said my wife.

"Three women to tie a scarf," I said.

Monsieur Bonnet, the proprietor of the hotel, waited for us at the station and drove us to the hotel. The word that comes readily to mind when I think of Beynac is picturesque. It is an overflogged word, the standby of guidebooks, but at Beynac it recovers its freshness and means what it stands for. The village is built alongside the Dordogne. The castle of Beynac is on top of the rocky hill, a huge, fine castle of the thirteenth century. It seems to hang on the edge of the rock, a grim yet appropriate shadow. Beynac was one of the four great baronies of Périgord. Nowadays it caters for the tourists and paddlers of canoes who come in summer. Though the village is tourist-conscious it does little for the tourist apart from trying to overdo the angle of picturesqueness, for which there is no reason whatever. We were well before the tourist season, yet the village made an effort to wake from its winter slumber and become heavily picturesque.

We were so delighted by the village, the castle and our dear Dordogne that we didn't look round in the hotel, but left our luggage and went out. There is a road along the river and little steep alleys climb in the direction of the castle. We walked along the road and soon reached the end of the village. We turned back, climbed a steep path and found ourselves outside a café, which was at the end of a cul-de-sac. Before we reached the bar two women with several rows of false teeth and artificial grins rushed us into a picturesque room, a room, we perceived, used in summer for the purpose of inducing tourists to dance and, consequently, consume drinks. On the walls were enlarged photographs of happy tourist groups which had danced contentedly in the café. The inevitable attraction for tourists wasn't missing, either: between the photographs hung copper saucepans. They belong to a somewhat curious tradition; for tradition alone could believe that the stranger might think that he was graciously singled out to watch and savour the intimate life of the innkeeper. Otherwise there is no explanation for the copper pans and dishes in rooms which cater for those who come, pay, then go.

"Ah," said one of the women, "the tourist season has started."

"Ah," said the other woman, rubbing her hands, "so

early. Excellent. We are surely going to have an abundant season. What will you take? Perhaps a little Vieille Noix? A speciality, you know, of these parts."

"A very good speciality," said the first woman, ready to dart for the door and bring the Vieille Noix.

"We'll get a table cloth," leered her companion.

"Please don't bother," I said rather boorishly. "I don't like Vieille Noix. Besides, I drank it for years and years, but don't like it any more. You see, we live in Souillac. We've been living there for the last fifteen years. Don't you think," I said turning to my wife and pretending not to notice the vanished grins of delight, "it's too cold here? Let's go to the bar."

We went to the bar, where a commercial traveller and two masons were drinking. The tourist spirit of Beynac dozed off at once, and we were left in peace in the sleeping village.

The moon appeared, lit up the river, the castle, the rocks, and wormed her way into the narrow alleys. It was the honeymooner's dream. Romeo should have loved Juliet in Beynac, and would have been wafted on the moonbeams to the balcony. Still enchanted, we went back to the hotel. The food was good, food we already knew well: food of the Périgord; and before we turned in Madame Bonnet told us there were a few workmen in the house, but they would abstain from noise.

We awoke in the morning to the din of hammering all round us—the room was as cold as the deep winter sea. We tried to ring the bell, but no bell was working. I put on my dressing-gown: in the passage it was colder and the hammering louder. I found the proprietor's daughter, who explained there was no heating in the hotel. The dining-room, however, would be specially heated for us. We were the only guests in the hotel. Bathroom? The workmen were in the bathroom. She would bring us a jug of hot water.

"Anyway," my wife said to me, "we are staying only for three days."

"But the hammering," I said. I was working hard at the time on a novel.

"We'll get accustomed to that. The day after tomorrow is Sunday."

"By then," I sighed, "I suppose I'll miss the hammering."

After breakfast we went out. The wind blew, but it was warmer out of doors. The wind was blowing our enchantment away. Perhaps Romeo did better by staying where he was. We walked upstream, beside the river, which didn't let us down. Poplars and willows accompanied us to a bridge, which we crossed, and on the other side the wind seemed to blow from a large castle that looked like the ideal setting for a medieval film crowded with knights and damsels. I chatted with a solitary fisherman who told me proudly that Josephine Baker had a château in the vicinity. We moved downstream now; after a while we saw Beynac on the opposite side, went on and perceived there was no bridge in front of us. We had no map, and on we went, reached another medieval film set, vast enough to suit the taste of a truly ambitious film magnate, but still no bridge in sight. I stopped a man; he told me the only bridge on which we could cross over was a railway bridge about a mile away. The thought of crossing a railway bridge didn't appeal to me, but we didn't want to turn back, so on we went after he had assured us there was no train before noon. To make doubly sure I asked the woman at the bridge and she said the same. We then started to cross on the railway bridge. The wind was stronger.

I for one am abysmally ignorant of all sorts of things that

surround my daily life, such as telephones, radio, how the lift works and why the lift stops if the door is opened. Therefore it is understandable that I had never observed that railway bridges are covered with sand, the rails and sleepers are on sand, and the sand is deep. The wind blew the sand in our faces, my dog didn't enjoy the sand, and our progress was painful and slow. It was a single-track bridge. There was practically no room between railings and rails, though at intervals tiny balconies appeared; evidently they were for railway workmen in case a train came. The balconies inspired me with no confidence. Notwithstanding my abysmal ignorance, I was pretty certain that if a train came it would, so to speak, suck us in. And the thought of a train coming was paramount in my mind. It was impossible to hurry: the sand saw to that. The wind held us back too. The view from the bridge was surely superb: but I didn't see the view. It was an eternity; then at last we reached the other side. We rushed off the embankment like liberated souls.

"Thank God that's over," I said to my wife, and at that moment, like a nightmare one remembers the next morning, a goods train appeared and came slowly across the bridge.

A few weeks later in the Basque country somebody suggested to us a short cut through a railway tunnel. I just smiled.

The dining-room was heated for luncheon, the workmen were at rest, a girl and a youth were our sole companions, the young man holding her hand and she giggling profusely. She giggled when she was asked whether she wanted soup or hors d'œuvres, she giggled when the workmen began hammering again. A cheerful girl, and we left and climbed up to the castle. There is a good road leading to the castle, but we chose a steep lane. The castle was closed; thus I must rely on the indefatigable Augustus J. C. Hare, who said that the Salle des États is full of curious mural paintings. The view was of great beauty. The river seemed to have been halted by the wind which was gathering even more strength.

Unfortunately, medieval castles attract me only from a distance. If I am near to them and look at their angry proud stone, I well understand Cardinal de Richelieu for having many of them pulled down, though not because the stone didn't appeal to him.

A woman was herding goats near the castle. She walked behind them, knitting industriously. The goats went down a steep escarpment, the woman, still knitting, followed them. I couldn't have gone down that escarpment even in a sitting posture.

On our way down we saw a small house with the notice on the door: To Let. Irresistible; and I knocked on the door. A thin, comparatively young woman opened the door. She was in mourning. I asked her to show us the house, and first we were taken into a room which was full of wicker chairs and tables. The tables were as long as dining-room tables. On the walls were framed photographs, and one bad oil-painting, depicting, of course, the Dordogne. Near the window were two rocking-chairs. Then she took us to a smaller room, furnished in the same way—only the tables were smaller, and there was a huge sideboard too. We went upstairs with her. The bedroom was mostly a bed. It was a menacing bed, a bed for bad dreams.

"It is very comfortable," she said. A little later she said: "My husband was an invalid. He always said he'd never want to sleep in any other bed." There was no answer to that. "He died in December. The house is too big for me. That is why I want to let it. Not now, you know. For the summer season. It is very pretty here during the tourist season."

Out of sheer curiosity I asked her how much she wanted to let it for. The sum was staggering.

"A very comfortable house," she said, and we thanked her and left. That bed haunted me for some time.

By the time night came the wind had completely lost its temper. In the dining-room sat another guest: the inevitable commercial traveller. It seems to me that all the trains, roads, buses and hotels of France are studded with commercial travellers. I can't think of any French town or village without conjuring up at least two commercial travellers. They are well worth studying. There are the successful travellers, the ambitious travellers, and the dejected travellers who travel from Monday till Saturday because they can earn their living in no other fashion. No faith and no hope burn in them; they follow a routine out of sheer habit, observe nothing, enjoy little except their return on Saturdays. There are those who chat a lot, those who flourish their money, those who eat sparingly and quarrel about their hotel bills. One thing they have in common: success with women. So they say, at least. The moment they leave their families on Sunday evening or Monday morning they turn into lady-killers. It is difficult to resist the picture of the train leaving the station; the commercial traveller, who sits in the last compartment of the last coach, rises automatically and goes from compartment to compartment, and by the time he reaches the carriage behind the engine every woman has been seduced.

I stayed in my time in small villages where not a woman was to be seen either in cafés or streets. Yet next morning the commercial traveller would narrate his success of the evening before, and give unsolicited details of the voluptuous night he had spent with an adorable virgin. Perhaps with those stories they try to compensate themselves for having to rise early, travel to boring places and be treated without undue fervour by innkeepers. Their lives are ruled by the alarm clock, the railway time table; so why shouldn't they be allowed to imagine they aren't alone in lonely hotel beds?

"I am, monsieur, the representative of a new brand of apéritif."

"No thank you."

"Would you like to taste it, monsieur?"

"No thank you."

"Just one little glass."

"I don't drink in the morning," says the café proprietor haughtily, and the poor traveller, because he doesn't want to look entirely like a beggar, buys himself a drink. I witnessed such sad scenes frequently.

The traveller in our icy hotel was of the sad variety. He ate little, drank no wine, and looked away when my dog approached him, blew his nose and hurried through his dinner. Before he left the dining-room he turned to us and said: "I can't understand anybody coming here who isn't forced to."

"That," said my wife, "was quite unnecessary."

Our icy bedroom seemed to echo his words. Next morning the hammering was, if possible, more sustained. We didn't want to cross the railway bridge again, we didn't want to climb to the castle again, so we walked downstream, and soon we were in flat country where the wind took an unnecessary new lease of life. We marched for miles to kill the morning. We were surrounded by endless fields, few trees, and now and then a lorry would cut through the wind. We chatted of this, that and the other, but we both knew what was in the other's mind. Suddenly I said: "Right, we'll leave today."

"I couldn't stick it any longer," said my wife.

We hadn't the courage to ask the proprietor for the railway time-table. Taking it all in all it wasn't his fault. His was a summer hotel, and during summer the sun does the heating. He couldn't very well get the place repaired while it was full of guests. Therefore, logically enough, he had the work done in winter. And that, if one reflects, makes travel difficult for those who don't like the lusty, teeming holiday-makers. Hotels are nowadays little else than abodes of summer tourists. Out of season the proprietors are dis-interested, they have made their money during the season, they hardly have a staff left, and for the traveller in search of solitude, only hotels in towns will remain, and perhaps he doesn't like towns more than he does crowds.

We went to the nearest café, where we discovered there was no train before the following morning. By then the notion of spending another night at Beynac had become worse than repugnant. We couldn't envisage it; in fact, it was out of the question even if the alternative was to leave on foot. The woman in the café was full of sym-pathy. Hers was the sympathy of the competitor: it would have been different if we had wanted to leave her establish-ment. That would have been sacrilege and a sign of folly. To leave somebody else's hotel or restaurant or bar is the right thing to do. No hotel, no bar, no restaurant is as good as your own. In the profession to which the café keeper and the hotel proprietor belong there are no doubts, no qualms—if they were ham actors they couldn't be more sure of themselves. The sympathetic woman told us she knew a young man who, provided he was handsomely rewarded, would drive us anywhere. I said we wanted to go to Bergerac. She telephoned him and he said he would come and fetch us in an hour's time.

The cold was surpassing itself; the Dordogne seemed to be expecting seals which had found the Arctic too tepid; and full of remorse, on account of our bold yet somehow treacherous decision, we returned to the hotel. I mumbled something to the effect that friends who were expecting us over there—I pointed in a westerly direction—had to leave earlier than expected, and we, because we didn't want to miss them, would have to leave at once.

"You will," said the proprietress, "retain a bad memory of our hotel."

"Nothing of the sort," I said, and heaved a sigh of relief, for the taxi had arrived.

We drove out of Beynac with the wind almost rocking the castle. We drove along a road, twisting and windy, till we reached Bergerac. Vineyard followed vineyard, and the country was flat. Bergerac is again a town which makes one feel that provincial life should continue—provided it isn't altogether stagnant—without one's presence. There are the cafés: the Grand Café with marble-topped tables, plenty of gilded looking glasses, the blowsy, old, ill-tempered cashier and a few customers. There are other sorts of cafés with red walls, red chairs, neon lights and bottles of Coca Cola. The young men of the town frequent these cafés, laugh, shout, and try to squeeze a kind of non-existent metropolitan gaiety from the sad provincialism which surrounds them. More to the point are the shops that sell seeds and agricultural implements, and perhaps a wandering peasant loiters before the shop window. Furniture shops abound. Imitation Henri II furniture stands for antiques; beds and wardrobes in the latest style of Messrs. Levithan hold the eyes of girls who hope to get married some day to a post office official. One is surprised and somewhat disappointed that there is no room in such a town for Timothy White's or the Fifty Shilling Tailors. The car parks are crowded, and as evening arrives so the cars leave. Soon the desolation of the car parks falls into line with the empty streets—the lights go out around nine o'clock.

We had one desire: to find a heated hotel. The mournful

silence of the town was brushed aside, the bill of fare displayed on the door of the best hotel in the main square left us unimpressed, notwithstanding the confit d'oie, foie gras, galantine de dinde and truffles with every course. We wanted a warm room. The hotel proprietor was in the hall. He received me graciously. He had large rooms, small rooms, rooms with bathrooms and rooms without them. The food, he told me proudly, was excellent.

"Are the rooms heated?" I asked.

"Heated?" he said surprised. "But, monsieur, it is warm, it is the middle of March, surely you don't expect heating at this time of the year."

I thanked him and went out into the windswept cold dusk. The car took us to the station, where we paid the driver, and the driver, with that admirable French gift, ceased to be the paid driver and stood us a drink. Then I stood him a drink, and he wanted to give back half the fare because we had come in vain to Bergerac. We had another drink at the station buffet, and he left us to visit the girl he was courting.

The auto-rail, or Micheline, was leaving at nine for Bordeaux. I bought our tickets, and it is worth recording that in the unfriendly first half of March we found no heated hotel between Souillac and Bordeaux.

We dined near the station in a restaurant which catered mostly for commercial travellers. The food was good and inexpensive. It is worth recording too that when in doubt it is preferable to dine in a restaurant in the vicinity of the station rather than to try out an unknown, more sumptuous looking restaurant in the centre of the town. Those which call themselves Auberge or Relais or Hostellerie and have, to boot, an olde worlde appearance should be avoided. Usually the food isn't good and prices are exorbitant.

The auto-rail left, two tired, podgy children whim-

pered, a man snored, a woman fell asleep over the Jardin des
Modes, and we reached Bordeaux towards midnight. Bordeaux is the other capital of south-western France. It was
explained to me in Souillac that if I studied the inhabitants
carefully enough I would soon guess by their habits who
preferred Bordeaux and who went to Toulouse. I am always
willing to study, and reached the probably erroneous conclusion that Toulouse was the public bar, whereas Bordeaux catered for the regulars of the saloon bar. The hotel
at Bordeaux awaited us with its warmth; but by then Souillac was far in the distance, and south-western France had
lost its meaning for me.

And the following winter I came again to Souillac, alone
because my wife had remained in England. My stay began
with sunshine, though only in the afternoons; for it took
till noon for the sun to rid the town of wet mist. The poplars were like elves in the sunshine and seemed ready to
dance away. There were days when I was the only guest in
the Grand Hôtel. My dog and I went for long walks, the
poplars accompanied us and the Dordogne flowed fast.
Towards the end of February the weather deteriorated, and
in March I went to Paris to meet my wife. We came back to
Souillac and we were now decided to visit Auvergne. Pierre
Betz took infinite trouble over planning our journey. We
were to start out for Aurillac on the fourteenth of April. It
was raining heavily. The morning of the thirteenth my wife
fell ill. Soon she had to be taken to the hospital in Gourdon.

That hospital defied nightmares. If a poor woman of the
district got ill she took her children with her to the hospital, because often enough there was nobody at home to
look after them. The hospital was full of noisy, screaming
children, and some sick people had brought their dogs.
The dogs on the second floor barked at the dogs on the
first—luckily there was no third floor. When I took my

wife in the decrepit ambulance to the hospital I was asked
whether I wanted to stay in the same room with her. There
was a second bed in the room.

Gourdon is at its best a sad, desolate town on top of a
hill, the plaything of winds. In the course of my daily
visits to the hospital I came to know the life of the town
only too well, provided one could call it life. Most of the
day the streets were empty, so were the cafés, and if I, the
solitary visitor, walked along the streets, windows opened
and eager faces appeared. Eyes brightened by curiosity
followed me as I went to or came from the hospital.

Gourdon is the seat of the sous-préfet. He lives in a
pleasant seventeenth-century house, a house one would
more expect to see in central France. At the time of my
wife's illness the sous-préfet was a charming, helpful young
man. He had his worries; for he had got into trouble with
the Communist Party. One of the employees at the hospital was an active Communist, and because he was a man
of strong personality ruled the hospital. He refused to obey
the orders of his superiors, believing nobody would dare to
discharge him. The sous-préfet suspended him. The Party
made a martyr of him, and in a nowadays no longer
original fashion declared him a victim of warmongers. A
peace meeting was called for the following Sunday. The
sous-préfet was in a difficult position. If he took drastic
measures and trouble ensued, even though he might be
praised for his action by the Minister of the Interior, the
minister wouldn't relish a storm in the Chamber, nor
political consequences which could perhaps rock the
government. It was a delicate situation. Came Sunday: the
town was full of the Garde Mobile, but the men in black
stood discreetly in courtyards and were to be called in only
if the crowd got out of hand. On Sundays the train service
to Gourdon was of no help to me, so a friend drove me

over. In the main thoroughfare we were stopped by Communists.

"Don't you know," said one of them, "that no car is allowed today into Gourdon?"

"We are demonstrating today," said another. "Please turn back."

"You aren't gendarmes," I said. "Therefore you have no right to stop us."

"We have."

"Think it over, you haven't."

It was a polite, almost affable conversation. He thought it over, his comrades thought it over and they reached the logical conclusion that I wasn't in the wrong. They let us go on, and, as far as I know, there was no incident at the peace meeting. The suspended employee was eventually dismissed.

My wife was very ill. The kindness of the people of Souillac was deeply moving. They went to Gourdon to see her; they went to their farms on the plateau to pick her flowers; and even the ticket puncher at the station would ask me on my return whether madame was any better. She wasn't. Towards the end of May she took leave of Souillac. She couldn't move any more, and all the people she had known came to the station in the hope that they could be of help. She was transported back to England, where she died in June. I received letters and telegrams from Souillac, a town we had discovered but by accident. Both in the *Dépêche* and the *République* touching articles appeared on *la mort de Madame de Polnay*, and came a morning when the good folk of Souillac rose early, and traipsed to the church with the three cupolas where Mass was offered up for the peace of her soul.

Chapter Two

SOUILLAC REVISITED

I

AT Uzerche one begins to lose one's belief in the imminent end of the world. Fire, destruction, envy and hatred seem to have fallen back, notwithstanding that the Paris–Toulouse express is no longer the fast train which hurried across the plains on the other side of Limoges. Viaducts, bridges, tunnels and the twisting railway line modify its speed. A hill appears with a château on the top. It has no garden, no park, no fences, and stands on the hilltop as though a giant had taken it from his pocket, put it down, gone away, forgotten it and hadn't sent anybody to look for it. Clear streams flow beside the railway embankment, tunnel follows tunnel and long stretches come with no sign of life.

It was a sunny day, the first day of sunshine and clear sky of the rainy May of 1951. It was the sort of warm sun that surely tickles the dead. They yawn, stretch themselves, smile and wait—in the evening as the sun goes down they perceive it isn't yet the Day of Judgment, and sleep on.

It was hot in the dining-car. A middle-aged, desiccated woman sat facing me. She had cold, calculating blue eyes, which reflected the figures her mind was adding up. Now and then she smiled: perhaps she had reached a pleasing number. A rivulet, narrow and clean, kept the train company for a few minutes. The woman opened her bag, took out pencil and paper, scribbled a few figures, gazed at them, folded the paper, and put it carefully among the mass of papers and documents most Frenchwomen carry in their

62

bags. The rivulet turned into a river, the stones in the river-bed could be counted one by one, and suddenly the river was gone. Shortly after a tunnel received the train, and as we came out on the other side I saw a factory at the bottom of a steep hill. A huge dark pipe connected the factory with the hilltop. Through that pipe rushed the water to turn the wheels of the factory. We met the river again farther on.

The woman looked out but her eyes took in nothing. In a little while she asked me whether I was going on business to Toulouse. I said I was going to Souillac, and from Souillac would move on to Auvergne. As a tourist? she inquired. No, not even as a tourist. Perhaps, she suggested, monsieur wanted to buy a property. One could find cheap properties near Sarlat. I said I didn't want to buy any property. She lost interest in me, though before she left the dining-car she wished me bon voyage.

Her place was taken by a large, bespectacled industrialist from Toulouse who drank quantities of beer. He had heavy eyes, a heavy jaw, and spoke ponderously of collars and shirts. He was a giver. He gave me everything he had accumulated in the course of his life; advice, maxims, epigrams, theories and the address of his shirt-maker in Paris. A bewildering amount of useless information sprouted from him—but givers give for the fun of it. He browbeat me into taking whatever he fancied out of his, to me, useless store.

"Don't forget," he said, "the shirt-maker is in the rue Verneuil, and the chemist who has that wonderful cure for ulcers is in the rue Monsieur le Prince."

He got off at Brive, leaving, as it were, the dining-car littered with his gifts.

Brive is no favourite of mine. It is a dismal town, though frequently visited by the Souillagais. The year before my dog had disgraced himself on market day by chasing a pig.

He did bring the town to life but was heartily cursed for it. Arthur Young didn't think much of Brive either. He came to Brive in 1787. The night before he reached Brive he had dined at Donzenac, still excited by the royal stud at Pompadour. Between Donzenac and Brive he met "the first maize, or Indian corn." Of Brive he said: "The view of Brive from the hill is so fine, that it gives expectation of a beautiful little town, and the gaiety of the environs encourages the idea; but on entering, such a contrast is found as disgusts completely. Close, ill-built, crooked, dirty, stinking streets, exclude the sun, and almost the air from every habitation, except a few tolerable ones on the promenade." Many of the crooked, stinking streets are gone, their place taken by soulless, straight streets flanked by equally soulless houses, which remind one of some of the poor suburbs of Paris. There are the uglier houses of the well-to-do, houses trying to be a mixture of Bauhaus, Provençale and Basque. Depressingly hideous houses; and during one of my brief visits to Brive I walked past such a building in the company of a charming woman of Souillac.

"What a beautiful house," she sighed. "I should like to live in a house like that some day."

"It's ugly," I said.

"Perhaps you are right," she said after she had looked again. "The front door shouldn't be green. It should be red."

Taste is admittedly an acquired quality. Children, for instance, have practically none. The simple life of my friend resembled in many ways the life of a child.

That indefatigable traveller Augustus J. C. Hare would have agreed neither with Arthur Young nor with me. But Hare was a Victorian enthusiast. He found the town pretty, admired the handsome houses; the crooked streets of Young became, for that fin-de-siècle traveller, winding

streets with admirable old houses. He praised too the rebuilt church of St. Martin. At the edge of the town is the
grotto in which St. Anthony of Padua stayed for a while.
To anyone who wants to study at close quarters the
mournful, heavy sadness of a thriving French provincial
town I warmly recommend Brive; yet many of my Souillagais friends assure me that if they want to have the time of
their lives they go to Brive.

The station is vast, and albeit it is on the electric line of
Paris–Toulouse, the smoke and noise of the shunting steam
engines give one the impression that the station is far up in
northern France. At three o'clock the train left Brive. A
bearded old man sat now facing me. A cheerful old fellow
who giggled for his own benefit, blew his nose regularly,
and between his lips was stuck a yellow, wet cigarette end.
He coughed it out before we reached Souillac.

The run between Brive and Souillac is familiar to me.
The train winds its way through tunnels and across viaducts. The line is on the top of the plateau, the land looks
uninhabited and wild. It was patronised by the Maquis
during the war. A thin man, his face grey, his eyes black,
joined our table. He was also from Toulouse but wasn't in
business. We chatted, and I whipped my hobby-horse,
namely I observed that sport had become a merciless enemy
of the arts.

"Take Souillac," I said. "Rugger, rugger, rugger.
That's all one hears, that's all they think of."

"You are perfectly right," he said. "The moment you
cross the Loire it is rugby, rugby, rugby. But it is different
in Toulouse, vastly different."

"Oh, is it?" I asked hopefully.

"Yes, you can take that from me. You never hear the
word rugby. We all play association football."

"I see."

The train reached the long viaduct, a section of which had been blown up by mistake by the Maquis during the Allied advance. At the end of the viaduct was the station of Souillac. The three cupolas of the church appeared, and the local drunk, who daily waits for the Paris express, was in the door of the buvette. When I had left Souillac nearly eight months ago he was at the station, drunk. Now he was drunk. It seemed to me as though he was the one man who had succeeded not only in beating time but in discarding it altogether. We shook hands. It was hot, the sun was half-way to Cieurac and the light was harsh. The drunk held my hand. The train moved off slowly—not slowly enough to escape the drunk's attention.

"Look out," he shouted, dropping my hand, "the train is going. Hurry, or you'll be left behind." He waved his stick, ran beside the train, and two railway workmen laughed uproariously. He became desperate as the train gathered speed; in fact, it was going at full speed by the time the last coach left the station. It was a touching thought that in his timeless, fuddled brain he imagined that I was travelling from one distant place to another distant place, and, having caught sight of him, jumped out of the train to shake his hand, and was ready to miss the train so great was my pleasure at being with him.

"Now what will you do?" he asked anxiously. "I suppose you will have to remain in Souillac."

I walked towards the town: it was like coming home. I waved to the driver of the Poste Rurale, I exchanged a few words with the waitress of the Bellevue. The saddler jumped off his motor-cycle, we shook hands and he asked: "How was your trip to England?"

The modern houses hid the château of Cieurac. Now I knew that the short cut to the centre went past the cemetery—now that I had come to Souillac alone, I had learned to disregard the flowery statement about the Dordogne breaking free from the grip of the mountains at Souillac to flow free and gay towards the plains of Périgord, for I had seen the river in the iron clasp of the mountains near Beynac. I had also learned that the Dordogne, in common with many other French rivers, dies many deaths. Each hydro-electric dam is a fresh grave. When the good fairies gave France her rivers, the bad one came at the end and declared they would be too fast in winter and too shallow in summer. Hence the dams, which aren't so much a fluvial matter as a case of electricity. I reached the cemetery and there stood the man whose wife had died. He stood still beside the grave. I reached the Grand Hôtel, now without Madame Couderc. I was received by Monsieur Couderc and Madame Berthe the manageress. The servants were the same. I should, I suppose, have gone at once to the church to see the Prophet Isaiah in order to ascertain that he was still coy and still flaunted his posterior. Betz came round and I sat with him and Monsieur Couderc. Two good friends; and I didn't bother to go up to my room, which the maids knew precisely how to arrange for me. Even a blanket was waiting for my dog Jamie. But Jamie wasn't with me: he was in quarantine in England. He was paying for his days of glory in France.

I heard all the news. A collection had been started for new church bells. The tin-like, hollow sound of the old bell would soon be replaced by gay peals. In a pamphlet the curé had written urging the Souillagais to contribute handsomely to the new bells. He used this phrase: "The souls of the people of Souillac thirst for new bells." An old woman had died since my last stay; a young man was dead too; an old man had had his third stroke but was recovering, in fact was playing poker again; and soon there would be the general elections. But Souillac was taking it all calmly. I saw an electioneering poster of the Communist Party urging the voters to fight Hitler. Little had changed in Souillac. I strolled as far as the mill and was surprised because I knew so few faces. Memory is prone to exaggerate. I had to admit that I was acquainted with only a small number of the inhabitants. From the distance of England their number had seemed immense. Next morning the siren went at noon. At least I knew the faces of the howling dogs. It was the same siren too.

In the afternoon I sat at my window and looked out on the Promenades. The sky was blue, it was agreeably hot, but I saw little of the sky owing to the dense foliage of the plane trees. From the hotel terrace English shrieks of delight mounted towards the leaves: a couple from Newcastle had discovered that the couple from Sunderland had met Auntie Kitty of Hull. The tourist, I reflected, is intrinsically the person who longs for home. "We were," I can hear the tourist say, "on the top of Mont Blanc, and guess what happened? We ran into the Saunders." It must be said in his favour that he is a large-hearted man; for he gives much, yet takes little. He gives one the description of his house at home, of the street in which he lives, and is ready to hand one, so to speak, in front of a Gothic abbey, the red brick town hall of his native place. He gives generously, and the Dordogne can flow freely because he doesn't want to take it away in his memory.

The delighted shrieks of the tourists were drowned by the drum of the town crier of Souillac. In some towns the town crier sports a bugle. In Sarlat I saw the town crier blow his bugle, but not a sound issued. The Souillac drum, however, is loud and the town crier wears spectacles. When he had ceased to beat his drum he announced that the funeral of a local dignitary would take place tomorrow morning at nine-thirty, fresh sardines had reached the fishmonger, and tonight a film would be shown at the cinema by courtesy of the Communist Party. The town crier mounted his bicycle, to which the drum was tied, and pedalled off. On the wall encompassing the hotel terrace sat the rugger enthusiasts, the boys from the Collège Technique, waiting for the sports papers. Some of them circled round slowly on their bicycles chatting, or whistling when they had nothing to say. Recently a man of forty-two had joined them, a married man with two children; nevertheless, he giggled boyishly in their midst. If it came to shouting he shouted as loud as they. A man, evidently, in revolt against maturity.

Suddenly the young men forgot their true vocation. The sports papers, which they await with the same trepidation with which in bygone days instalment readers feared the impending death of Little Nell, were also forgotten. Eyes were focused on the garage next to the Banque Populaire. In front of the garage stood a four-horse-power Renault, the beetle of French roads. A tall man, dissatisfied with some repair done to his car, gesticulated wildly, shouted abuse and appeared as ridiculous as one does when one has lost one's temper. The garage keeper laughed, the sports lovers laughed, and the hot sun beat down on the trees and the Route Nationale. The irate owner of the car, rolling down the slope of his temper, became, if possible, even more angry. A gendarme was bicycling along the road, bicycling slowly, partly because it was hot and chiefly because he wanted to have brief chats with passing acquaintances. The irate owner stopped the gendarme. Everybody was hooting with laughter, and the little scene was the making of everybody's afternoon, the car owner, of course, excepted.

The people of south-western France have an almost oriental appreciation of the ridiculous, and to laugh at one who has no control of his temper is part and parcel of the enjoyment of life. Life, they maintain, should be enjoyed. One laughs if one wants to enjoy life, and one should hurry under no circumstances. The price of hurrying is death, which, the more one hurries, the sooner one reaches. So the boys didn't hurry back to the college, but sat and laughed at the discomfited man who, after the gendarme had left, drove away, trying to look haughty but without success.

Now and then it happened to me in Souillac that I had an appointment with some acquaintance and the appointment wasn't kept. No rudeness or thoughtlessness was implied. It simply meant that if it were the other way round he would know how to spend or waste his time agreeably. Besides, if it is agreeable it can't be wasted.

I left my room, crossed the Promenades and sat down outside the Café de Paris. Both the Café de Paris and the Café du Quercy were emptier than they had been during my last tour; and every time I return to Souillac I find the cafés less frequented. The cost of living has risen, but even so I don't believe it is so much a sign of higher prices or dwindling incomes as a deepening lack of desire to spend money. One spends if one feels things are going well . . . but I needn't pursue the argument to its conclusion. I sat alone in the café with Madame Sabatié and her daughter. A woman friend of theirs came to join them, then a commercial traveller followed. All he wanted was to write a letter. He ordered no drink, on the other hand he asked for pen and ink. Paper he had. An English tourist entered the café with a camera, a long nose, and he was walking on tiptoes. He must have considered that a swinging gait. He came as eagerly as if he were on his way to a darts match at his local.

He stopped before me, took from his pocket a battered matchbox, fingered it deftly, anxiously, because he didn't want the occupant of the matchbox to escape; and, as I had feared and suspected, a Colorado beetle was in the box. He danced back a step, pushed his palm forward for the beetle to approach within my ken. It was a horrid looking beetle.

"Is this," he asked half in a whisper, "a Colorado beetle?"

That was the first Colorado beetle I had ever seen, or, probably, noticed. I shouldn't have known it was a Colorado beetle but for the matchbox. A few years ago I had read in the papers of a man who was apprehended at Dover with a Colorado beetle. The beetle was found in a matchbox; the magistrate had no kind words for the culprit; and since then matchboxes are associated in my mind with Colorado beetles.

"It is," I said.

"I thought so at once," said the tourist, all anxiety gone. "In fact, I was convinced it was. Thank you very much, very kind of you." He beamed at me. "I had a hunch that you might know. Thank you, thank you. Curious things Colorado beetles." He thought for a second. "Very exciting."

He put the matchbox in his pocket and tiptoed off triumphantly. His holiday was made. For him the Dordogne could be shallow in summer and fast in winter; the Dordogne could have remained, as it had been in the Tertiary Age, on the plateau; but he had his Colorado beetle, thus his holiday was a success.

"Why did he show you that beetle?" asked Madame Sabatié.

"Because he likes it," I said.

She shook her head. The tourist, whom I could still see through the window, stopped here and there to look at his treasure, then he disappeared in the direction of the common where my friend lives. My friend is an eight-year-old gipsy boy.

He lives in a caravan with his mother and sister ; the father died of consumption, though before his death he had in a fuddled state overlaid one of his children, for there was little space in the caravan. The child died. The mother, tall, dark, gaunt and dirty, is a drunk too. She goes about Souillac with a certain austere dignity, keeping to herself, seldom smiling. My friend is eight years old; he is fair and modest, but I fear his modesty will wear off in time. Monsieur Couderc pays for his weekly cinema matinée ticket: he bothers him on no other occasion. Somebody else gives him food, here a kind person buys him a cake, there a friendly soul gives him a few sweets. Our friendship is of two years' standing: our dogs brought us together. He has a dog, ungainly, scruffy and given to shrill barking. My friend admired my dog and suddenly had an idea. He came to the Café de Paris with his dog; the dog was led on a string.

"Monsieur," he said, pulling towards me the somewhat frightened dog, "I should like to swop dogs. I give you mine and you give me yours. Mine is a very good dog."

"Out of the question," I said.

"But, monsieur," he pleaded, "mine is a big dog, yours is a small dog." He showed with his hands how small my dog was. "It is you who would profit by it. Look how big mine is. Yours—well, one can hardly see him."

"That's not the point," I said. "My dog's been with me for seven years."

As Souillac doesn't lack the virtuous either, it has been suggested that he and his sister should be sent to an institution. To live in a caravan with a drunken mother was considered practically indecent by the virtuous. Luckily, nothing came of it. Why, said the notaire, should freedom

be taken from them? Why, I asked, should he succumb to
the bane of our age, namely that others should decide the
form of happiness we should pursue according to their rules
on the road appointed by them? My gipsy boy is happy in
spite of the rain which often pours on the stuffy caravan,
happy in spite of the rags he wears. In the evenings he likes
to stand in the company of his sister in front of the Grand
Hôtel, and to watch the hotel guests eating the sort of food
that will never come his way makes him happy; and if an
acquaintance comes out of the hotel his faint little voice
pipes up, "Bonsoir, monsieur," and he is doubly happy.
His hand-to-mouth existence keeps him from meanness. A
visitor once gave him a sum of money which for him was a
king's ransom. I asked him shortly after how he had spent
it. Cakes for himself, cakes for his sister, and what was left
he gave to his mother because she hadn't had money for
wine for the last three days.

Another advantage of that free, roaming gipsy boy is that
he is an outlet for the urge of charity, an urge that nowadays
is systematically dammed up in most bosoms. The hand
withers in our age, for it has lost the habit of giving.

He came to see me soon after my arrival. I gave him some
pennies, and the following morning when we met again I
inquired how he was doing at school. He said he couldn't
take down dictation because he had no pen.

"Why," I asked, though it was, strictly speaking, no
business of mine to ask, "didn't you buy a pen with the
money I gave you?"

"I prefer cakes, monsieur," he said, and I saw his point.

His love of cakes can also be his undoing. He had a little
money, it was a Monday and a number of Sunday cakes
were left over in the cake shop. Bargains; and I saw him go
off heavily loaded with cakes. In the evening he ruefully
confessed that he had been copiously sick.

"You should eat fewer cakes," he was told.

"I can't: I am too fond of them."

He is a cautious boy if no cakes are involved. He told me he wouldn't travel in a ship, on an aeroplane or mount a motor-cycle. They frighten him. Moreover, he has no wish to die. The dead, he must think, don't eat cakes. His mother had done comparatively well during last winter. A man came to Souillac and bought chicken feathers at a high price. The mother found him chicken feathers, found as many as he wanted, and the coming of the man and the going of the feathers became father to the rumour that the Americans needed chicken feathers for atom bombs. Thus the mother found her niche in the cold war.

"Do you like nightingales?" the boy asked me one evening when the nightingales were singing somewhere on the other side of the common. "I am told, monsieur, they make very good eating."

In May the nightingales sing sweetly in Souillac. They sing like the troubadours whom they outlived to carry on their tradition, and carry in their song, as it were, the troubadours' hearts. They sing so loudly that their song walks in and out of one's dream, and, surprisingly enough, makes the dream uneasy, and it is as if the nightingales were delivering a warning. And the year before, when I used to go to the hospital of Gourdon every day, they sang perhaps louder, became masters of my dreams, but I refused to listen to their warning.

One stuffy evening there stopped before the Grand Hôtel a huge snail on four wheels: an American car. An earnest, bespectacled American got out, and as I was the only person sitting on the terrace he put his question to me. At what time did the famous nightingales of Souillac begin to sing? He waited eagerly for the reply. Such a question is irresistible.

"At ten-thirty," I said.

The weather was becoming warm, the sun was harsh and heavy. There is no spring to speak of in south-western France. Summer, as I have said elsewhere, arrives like a burning railway engine. It bursts in tactlessly and seems to stay for good. Autumn, however, is the compensation for the lost spring; and as one who saw the four seasons in Souillac, I should say the end of September and the first half of October are the best days in that region. The heat of the summer sun is helped along by the arid Causses. The Causses begins at Roc-Amadour. The comparatively poor land above Souillac is called the plateau, and it would annoy the Souillagais if it were confused with the Causses. In the Causses nothing grows. It is waste land; alone the wind of winter and the sun of summer frequent it. Also the Maquis during the war—not the Germans. The Causses seems to gain ground, and its aridity works towards the decline in population of the district. The old peasants till stubbornly the ungrateful earth; their children, however, give up the fight the day they are free to leave. They drift into over-populated towns, fill the overcrowded slums, and the desert increases with every departure. The parents die, their houses crumble, the Causses takes over—another victory of our age. On the road to Cahors one can see another sort of desert. About fifty years ago there were long stretches of vineyards to which the phylloxéra put an end. The vines weren't replanted; only a few sheep and goats live in that desolation.

Not far from the Causses an edifying experience came my way. It became known in the district that I intended to write a travel book of sorts. The commercially minded applauded the idea, others took a poor view of it, for they thought that I would write of their trips to hotels and strolls in the evenings beside the Dordogne. They were convinced that their private lives were of perennial interest.

Some believed I would fill a book with observations on stones, soil and crops: the usual paraphernalia of travel books—their idea of travel books, and they pitied me. However, the edifying experience came from a purely commercially minded person. Monsieur Lavergne, the president of the Syndicat d'Initiatives, informed me he had been rung up by a hotel-keeper who asked him to let me know that he would be pleased if I visited his hotel; in fact, he had invited me to luncheon, and he, Lavergne, would drive me there in his car. The hotel-keeper, though a Frenchman, had lived for a long stretch of time in England, and that, thought Lavergne, would certainly be a bond between us. He added the hotel was a transformed château, and he believed I should get a good meal. He for one hadn't been to the hotel before. Pierre Betz accompanied us.

By the end of May the landscape is cabbagy, the lines of the trees are lost in the thick foliage. Nonetheless, the landscape isn't weighed down: the poplars lift it. The air was filled with heat, the sky was laden with heavy clouds. My friends were both worried about the hotel-keeper inviting them to stay for luncheon. That, they thought, wouldn't be fair, since, after all, he had bargained for me alone. Their fears were promptly assuaged, for when we arrived at the château the hotel-keeper didn't even ask them to have a drink. It was noon, the time of day when anybody within earshot is asked in France for a drink. Betz and Lavergne left me. They would fetch me at four o'clock, four hours being ample for the abundant meal they believed I would be given. In that part of the world one eats slowly and copiously.

The proprietor insisted on speaking English to me, showed me round the premises and praised himself effusively. It was a château which had been rebuilt at the turn of the century, and bad taste had then swept France as thoroughly as England. It was furnished cheaply and pretentiously. The rooms, for some unilateral reason, were named after popular French writers of the last century. A little conversation persuaded me that he had named the rooms after the authors of the few books he had read; and he went on praising himself in English. I was thirsty: the best hour of the morning was rushing past without bearing me its wet offering. Since I considered myself his guest I couldn't very well ask him for a drink. Eventually he took me into the neglected garden, showed me a small torn net, said proudly: "We play deck tennis here," handed me his *livre d'or*, then asked whether one o'clock would suit me for luncheon.

"But I am completely at your disposal," I said. "Whenever it suits you."

"I hope," he said, "the appetite is good, because you will need a hearty appetite to eat the food we eat here."

He left me. I went and sat on the stone wall and gazed at the countryside: rolling hills, woods, glades, all encompassed by the distant horizon, partly swallowed by the dense heat. It was a pleasing extended view. It became too hot on the terrace; I walked about and the gardens were the realm not so much of neglect as of an unshakable lack of interest. At one o'clock my dapper host appeared. He took me to the verandah, where he ceased to be my host. There was a table laid for one person only. He assured me I would be served with the best meal I ever had. He had a surprise for me: meat. Yes, meat; and then I understood. In that land of plenty he catered with both eyes on the restrictions prevailing in England, believing everybody arrived famished from England, people who knew nothing of the French way of living and eating, who would be grateful for a meal a French railway worker would turn his back on. He explained it would be a simple meal because he despised extravagant restaurant cooking. What he liked and gave his clients was simple, healthy, decent home-cooked food.

"You will agree," he said, "that the sort of food they give around here is eyewash. In this house everything is home cooked."

"I don't think," I said with hatred in my voice, "that écrevisses flambées, foie gras, truffes sous les cendres, coq en pâte are eyewash."

He gave me the sort of smile one gives when sharing a joke. His wife appeared, and they stood over me, praised the food, ogled me, forcing, as it were, an alliance on me against France in general and the Quercy in particular because their food was home cooked. It is difficult to find tough steak in the Quercy: they, however, had done so successfully. Two vegs. were served with the hard bit of meat. Chips and boiled cabbage.

"It is home cooked," he said.

"I thought," I said almost trembling with anger, "that you had this flown from England."

They laughed. Oh, they were given to laughter. They knew a joke when they heard one. Besides, we were friends: we all knew where Oxford Circus was. The wine was mediocre; it was hot and I hated them. I saw them as the profiteers of another country's misery; I pictured them listening in to the nine o'clock news, and if the Minister of Food announced that the meat ration would be cut, gloating and contented they would cut their clients' meat portion in France. They were the righteous, the straight, the conscientious. Let nobody feel relief when he comes to the land of no restrictions. More butter? Certainly not. Why should one exceed one's butter ration just because one happens to be in France? None of that here, please. This isn't a black market hotel. Moreover, eyewash food isn't served on the premises: only decent home-cooked food which must be shared alike. I was of course exaggerating, but that was my only enjoyment.

"Do you get many French visitors?" I asked.

"We cater for the English," he said.

Four o'clock seemed as far as the end of the century. At long last it came with thunder and black clouds. Betz and Lavergne arrived and they understood the situation at once. I asked for my bill, the bill was presented, and I paid about double what I should have paid at the Grand Hôtel. We left, and the hotel-keeper told me before the door of the car closed that if I felt like wanting to eat a good meal again I should not hesitate to visit his establishment. Betz and Lavergne were furious. I, on the other hand, gloried in my liberty, so couldn't help laughing. In the end they both decided the man was a *pauvre malheureux* who understood nothing, and we discussed more congenial topics. They drove me first to Roc-Amadour. We went to the Hôtel Sainte Marie where they insisted on my eating foie gras because I must still be hungry. The hotel proprietor didn't let us pay because, he said, the other man had let down the profession. My friends weren't yet satisfied: they took me to a small village where we ate smoked ham. We ate plenty of ham; nevertheless, we stopped at two more villages. By the time we reached Souillac I felt heavy with food and had forgotten the importer of restrictions.

It was market day, the rain had stopped, and before a garage stood a brand new tractor. The evening sun shone on the shiny tractor and peasants flocked to it. They stood round it, admired it and the garage keeper smiled hopefully. One of the enraptured peasants stayed longer than the others: he couldn't tear himself away—evidently a buyer. When he left at last I overheard him say: "I liked those headlamps. So beautiful."

II

Souillac has three thousand and three inhabitants, Betz said: "Only the three matter." But, one could add, the three have probably left by now. For the Souillagais are on the move; each year a number drift away, and the number of those who drift away increases yearly. The balanced, unrapacious life doesn't seem to appeal to the young. They prefer to loiter in the industrial districts of Paris to fishing in lazy contentment beside the willows of the Dordogne. To cast a stone at them would, in many ways, be as futile as unjust. The books they read, provided they read books, the magazines which they certainly read— magazines dealing with film stars, glamour and gossip—the radio they listen to and the films they see turn them away from their somnolent, placid homes. But what turns them away with more force and reason is the low pay they receive in the few local factories. If they don't like the pay they can lump it, that is to say they must either leave the district or find themselves out of jobs. Naturally they go. Yet few of them are influenced by magazines, radio and films. They give them only the impetus. The impetus sends the cautious young men into government jobs which guarantee them a pension. Pensions have become the carrot of the French donkey. A mother would rather marry her daughter to a small post office official than, say, to a small, independent, struggling artisan. That can easily be understood. In France, and especially in the south and south-west, the fear of old age hardly exists. Old age is a goal, old age is the plum of life; for old age means peace, pension and a small plot; also rabbits and chickens. In old age one returns to one's village and one takes to fishing among the willows of the nearest river, which is an interesting thought: the young man who sets out from Souillac has as his aim the quiet life of Souillac after all.

There are those who don't have to wait for old age in order to enjoy a tranquil life. One example comes to mind, namely the *tripier*. The vendor of tripe makes his round every morning, the hot tripe in his little cart, a cart one finds usually before the cafés. He spoke to me of a friend who had made good in Paris. He came for a short visit with the trappings of Parisian wealth, an American car, a gold cigarette case, a noisy tie, and the beret had been exchanged for a felt hat. The rich man was filled with pity. He moaned over the poverty and simplicity of the tripe vendor's existence.

"I told him," said the vendor, ordering another round of drinks, "he can keep his money if it included the hustle and noise of Paris. If I go to Paris and stay for a couple of days I come back a sick, tired man. I don't want that kind of life. It isn't life. I prepare the tripe in the morning, I push my cart at the speed I want to, I stop for a drink whenever I feel like it, when I've sold the tripe I go home, eat a good meal, in the afternoon I go fishing or shooting, a game of cards in the evening, and nobody can harm me. I do as I like and don't have to hurry. Rich? Let him be rich." He thought for a moment. "Besides," he added "he has to get up, rich or not rich, on the first of January the same way as I, and goes to bed on the thirty-first of December the same way as I."

But let it not be imagined that life in Souillac is monotonous. The same evening I was sitting outside the Café de Paris, looking at maps of Auvergne, asking questions about Auvergne from those who had never been there. Incidentally, nobody seemed ever to have been to Auvergne. It was still hot, the heat as if screwed to the town. Abruptly I dropped the maps because a fight had begun outside the Communist café, a fight that had nothing to do with doctrine. Before the café sat a lover, and his mistress came to attack him in a fit of jealousy. He was a man of forty-five, whereas she was of the ripe age of seventy-eight. She sold cabbage in the market square and he, apparently, divided the proceeds with her. She had suspected him for some time, and the heat of the evening and of the drink in her must have decided her to have a showdown. She came rushing up and called him many names. She said what the better-off partner in a love affair is seldom loth to say, that is she kept him. She enumerated the small sums of money she had given him, she shouted the list of presents and food, and added her charm to the figure she reached. He took it first good humouredly; and that annoyed her. He chatted with the man who sat beside him, and she considered that the limit. She carried a bowl of soup: her supper. She was going to take it home before she had lost her temper. Now she hurled the bowl at the lover. It didn't hit him, but he hit her. The bowl lay in the gutter, the soup made a small pool, and above it stood the lover. He boxed her ears, punched her and his foot rose and it was preparing to kick her. The onlookers said, "Don't hit her too hard," and not a soul moved. She ran towards the public lavatory, stopped and shouted she would keep him no more.

"She'll think it over," said someone to me. "She won't find another young man of forty-five very easily."

The local wits call her *la grande amoureuse du siècle*.

Last year there was another lovers' tiff, but that one ended in tragedy. The woman was tiresome and married to a peasant. She nagged him. The moment came when he felt he'd had his share of her nagging and made up his mind to put an end to it. He was full of drink, went upstairs, got hold of her, dragged her to the window and threw her out.

Alas, it isn't an easy task to throw a struggling wife through a window. He was to find out the truth of that. She held on to him, wouldn't let go of him, thus he followed her, or probably they went out together. She fell on the soft dung heap, he on the hard surface of the court-yard. He broke his neck and died; she is still with us and is, so I was told, as tiresome as ever.

The next day was the last day of the sudden heat. I was taken to two villages which will remain bright in my memory as long as it lasts. The first village is called Turenne, often referred to as Turenne la Féodale. From that village hails the family of the great marshal. It forms half a circle round the hill and the houses go up the hillside to meet the château on the top. The castle till the Revolution was the seat of viscounts who exercised jurisdiction over a certain number of towns in the neighbourhood. The Romanesque church is of the thirteenth century, and Augustus J. C. Hare supplies the information that the village is five hundred and eighteen kilometres from Paris. It was impossible for me to think of Paris in that village wrapped in ageless serenity, surrounded by hills, valleys and woods spreading in every direction till the horizon gently clamps down on them. The peace of that village is as good an answer to the fear of annihilation as one could conjure up. From the castle one looks down on the houses of the village, and the pattern of the roofs remains unforgettable. The steep path is flanked by old houses, and what with the sun, the lizards and the old women in black, one feels one is deep in the south. Fearless ducks sat in the shade: none of them moved and I had practically to step over them. An old woman showed us round the castle. When we came into the vast stone-flagged hall she said: "This is where the master of the house usually plays bridge with his friends."

The second village, called Collonges, is red. The houses are built with red stones found in the local quarry. Every house is red. The church, which is Romanesque turning into Gothic, is red, and the light was red too. Like Turenne, Collonges was left to us by the courtesy of a more gracious age, which is blatantly untrue, for both villages have trembled as the hard wind of history frequently blew through them. Yet one wants to believe it was a more gracious and more peaceful age for the good reason that in our time the wind seems to blow too fast and too often. Besides, many of us cast more hopeful looks into the past than into the future, which, though possibly the wrong thing to do, has its charm, compensation and isn't futile altogether.

There is a gate in Collonges named the Gate of the Siren. Sirens could easily be imagined in that village. Near the gate is a well. The kind friends who took me to the village in their car were astonished when I explained to them that the water of that well was the entire water supply of the village. As if to illustrate my statement an old woman in black came to fetch a bucketful of water, which in all likelihood was the water for the evening, water for the family, the cow, the soup and for the fowls too. In the church the tablet of the dead of the 1914–18 war records over forty names. If one speaks of France, tries to explain and understand France, one should bear in mind those tablets; and every village, small or large, has its crowded tablet.

I was puzzled by the church. I had the impression that the Gothic and the Romanesque were built at the same time. They are entwined and the eye can't separate them. I asked a man about the church. I found him near the well and he exuded authority and learning.

"It's very simple," he said. "In that church at a given moment—I don't know when it was—the Catholics and the Protestants worshipped side by side. See?"

I didn't, but thanked him.

The heat held on for another day, and on that day I went to Roc-Amadour. Though this was my seventh visit to Souillac, I hadn't been to Roc-Amadour before. My loss —now I know that. It wasn't a matter of not finding time; time at Souillac is as abundant as water is rare in the Causses. I simply hadn't been. The first view one gets facing Roc-Amadour is of the village hanging, so to speak, on the side of the mountain, and the deep cauldron is like a deep green hole that somehow or other shouldn't be there because it is unexpected. It isn't a practical joke of nature but one of its superb surprises giving the lie to Oscar Wilde's remark about art and nature. Art couldn't afford a surprise on such an immense scale. The village caters for tourists and pilgrims, it is a beehive of picture-postcards and souvenirs. That is beside the point. The point is the Chapel of Our Lady of Roc-Amadour.

That statue of Our Lady is of great beauty, a black Madonna of Auvergne. The hundred and forty-three steps leading to the chapel are exposed to the hot sun, and the pilgrims, whose number is legion, pilgrims old and young, go up those steps, often on their knees in the torrid month of September, the month of the yearly pilgrimage. I know of an old woman, poor, and heavy with the wrinkles of age, who used to travel on foot from her hamlet forty miles away, slept in the open, reached Roc-Amadour, and then went up on her knees on the hard, hot steps stung by the sun, yet exulting with joy at last when she reached the chapel of the Miraculous Virgin. And before her through the ages had gone up on their knees to the shrine Henry II in 1170, St. Louis and his mother Blanche de Castille in 1244, Philippe II in 1271, Philippe le Bel in 1303, Philippe de Valois in 1324, Louis XI in 1443 and 1465; also St. Bernard and St. Dominique "followed by immense crowds."

The Black Prince pillaged the shrine, and then went to die of the pestilence at Martel.

The wooden statue of Our Lady of Roc-Amadour is a Romanesque Virgin of Auvergne. A manuscript at Clermont-Ferrand takes us to the birth of those statues. After the Normans had burned and looted Clermont its bishop Étienne rebuilt the town. The new cathedral was built by Aleaume, an architect and goldsmith. The bishop ordered Aleaume and his brother Adam to build a throne of gold, adorn it with jewels and put on it the effigies ''in fine gold of the Mother of God and Our Lord her Son'' sitting on her knees, and inside the statue the bishop put relics of the Virgin.

That, according to the chronicle, is the origin of the Virgins of Auvergne, and numberless Virgins were carved and sculpted all over Auvergne. Between Roc-Amadour and Saint-Flour I saw many of them. They are small, about eighty centimetres in height. They are, if one could use the expression, pre-primitive, for they were, so to speak, the beginning of any form of art—apart from architecture—of the Middle Ages in central France. Their realism is impressive. If one leaves the church and looks round in the square one sees a lot of faces with similar features. The statues were carved in oak or walnut. The Mother and Child are often black, like those of some Byzantine ikons. There are many theories concerning the black faces. One of them is that through the ages the faces were blackened by the smoke of incense and tapers. It is, however, noteworthy that some of the Virgins were painted black subsequently. Our Lady of Saint-Victor-de-Montvianeix is a good example. When the black paint was scraped off, delicately painted rosy cheeks were found under the black paint. In Auvergne a peasant woman gave me this explanation: ''Everybody who was born over there was black.'' And she

waved her hand in the direction of a distant hill—the sun
had risen from behind that hill in the morning. Perhaps the
most moving of the Virgins of Auvergne is Nôtre-Dame
de Marsat. The Virgins of Auvergne, to quote Marcel
Gromaire, have the smell of the earth, indulge in no chit-
chat, ask no questions and have no *crises de conscience*. They
possess, however, the sublime quality of true faith—the
faith of those who had carved them. And if one examines
them one understands why Romanesque, when it tried to
become subtle, had to give way to Gothic, in fact turned
into it.

I sat on the terrace of the Hôtel Sainte Marie. Beneath
me was the deep cauldron, yet my thoughts remained with
the steps and the statue of Our Lady. On those steps I had
felt the faith of those who had gone before me—the faith of
others can help one's own. In the Middle Ages Roc-
Amadour was one of the four principal pilgrimages with
Rome, Jerusalem and St. James of Compostella.

In the year 1166 was found a completely preserved body
under a rock in the Gorge d'Alzou, believed to be the body
of Zacchaeus, the publican of the Gospels, who, after the
death of his wife Veronique, had come to Gaul to build a
chapel in honour of Our Lady. It is held by other authori-
ties that it was the body of a hermit called Amadour. It is
more or less established there had been a chapel before the
body was found. Legend has it that Roland passed through
Roc-Amadour on his way to Spain. In the Miraculous
Chapel hangs a small bell, considered one of the oldest
bells in the western world. It dates from the seventh or
eighth century. According to the chronicles it rang by itself
whenever a miracle happened. The statue of Our Lady
is of the twelth century.

Troubadours often came as pilgrims to Roc-Amadour,
and around the year 1220 when a famous singer, one

Gautier de Coincy, sang in the chapel the praise of the Virgin, a taper of the altar, like a star, fell on his lute.

The road from Roc-Amadour to Souillac reminds one of a road high up in the mountains. It twists, and the vegetation, or rather the lack of it, on each side of the road gives a false impression of height, as though one was somewhere in the Pyrénées, yet one is seldom more than fifty or sixty feet above the level of Souillac.

The thread on which the heat hung tore, and on Saturday the rain came down. It came as if the clouds could supply unlimited water for the duration of the summer. It rained heavily, unyieldingly; and the lights went out every five minutes or so. In the course of the first winter I had spent in Souillac the lights went out too when it rained. Then the explanation was that there wasn't enough water in the lakes behind the dams. Now the answer was there was too much water. Apparently one can't satisfy the capricious dams. On Sunday it was still raining; and Sunday was my last Sunday at Souillac. I went to Mass, and a woman pushed a large white pram into the church: two infants slept in it. Now and then some of the dogs follow their masters to church.

A rainy Sunday is more or less the appropriate day to think of the past. The present was wet, and the future belonged already to Auvergne. For a long time Souillac had belonged to the Kings of England, and its background, historically speaking, is also the background of the two Hundred Years' Wars; and sitting in the Café de Paris that rain-darkened afternoon I asked one of the professors of the Collège Technique, Monsieur Laverdet, to make for me a summary of those wars purely from the angle of a Souillagais. Laverdet is a man of wit and learning; and next day he gave me his résumé, which I here translate, leaving it exactly as he wrote it.

The Quercy

A small province attached to Guyenne, belonging to the Prince of Aquitaine, fief of Eléonore d'Aquitaine. The capital was Bordeaux.

Souillac was a royal abbey.

Why England?

Eléonore d'Aquitaine, divorced wife of Louis VII, married Henry Plantagenet who became Henry II of England. In 1159 the possessions of Eléonore came under the suzerainty of the King of England (Normandy, Anjou, Aquitania, etc.).

The Wars

The Kings of France, whose policy was the unification of France, tried to suppress all the suzerainties of the Kings of England in France.

The Kings of England, in order to consolidate their possessions in France, decided to conquer the whole of France.

Hence the two Hundred Years' Wars.

Some facts

On the 23rd of February 1233 the Alliance of Roc-Amadour: seventeen feudal lords and towns decided to resist the English.

1345: Belcastel is taken by Henry of Lancaster, Duke of Derby.

1351: Souillac falls.

1369: Chandos and Robert Knolles take Roc-Amadour. The town is ordered to provide the English with the quantity of food fifty mules can carry.

1470: The Quercy is liberated, the English are massacred and their bodies thrown into the Dordogne.

Politics

It is only towards the middle of the fourteenth century that the French national spirit becomes evident. Previously it was but a case of fealty to the overlord.

7

Strategy

The English took and held key positions such as Belcastel, Creysse and Pinzac, thus they were the masters of the Dordogne. Each garrison consisted of about three thousand to four thousand men.

Tactics

When spring came the garrison troops, aided by the Routiers, sacked towns and held them to ransom.

Results

Pillage, arson, ruined harvests, poverty, rape, destruction, misery.

Advantage

Planting of vines, ordered by the English who already then were fond of drinks. Development of commerce, and the birth of the French national spirit.

Remains

Fortified castles and cemeteries of the English.

I thanked Monsieur Laverdet. Then we had a good laugh.

The Sunday ended as most of my Sundays end in Souillac with a game of poker. A suave man from Paris played with us. He played a good game and won. While he was present tempers were kept under control. When he left pandemonium broke out. They had all lost and now they accused one another of having helped the stranger to win. Why did you bid? You forced the bidding simply because you wanted the man from Paris to win. Purely to undo me you threw your hand in. I know why you bid like that.

Slowly the gamblers relaxed and tempers became more even; for what they had lost to the stranger they won back from me. That, however, was as it should be. The money I left behind at Souillac should keep my memory green.

I went to take leave of the church with the three cupolas, that Aquitanian Romanesque church and not Byzantine as I and a few more had liked to believe. The church was built on the site of a demolished Carolingian church of either the eighth or the ninth century. The tower, some think, is the original tower of the Carolingian church—others think differently. The church, it is said, was built in 1150—an arbitrary date, though probably not far wrong. But I had come to say goodbye; and I said goodbye to the Prophet Isaiah, to the sculptured legend on the tympanum of the monk Theophile who had sold his soul to the devil but was saved by the Mother of God, and, finally, to the curious, sculptured column of the seven capital sins. As I left the church I ran into one of the players of the night before.

"It broke my heart to see you lose," he said.

"Don't think too much of your broken heart," I said. "Think of mine. You see, I am leaving Souillac in an hour's time."

Chapter Three

AURILLAC

THOUGH it had been my intention for years to visit Auvergne, I knew mighty little of the land of Lafayette and Pascal. I knew it consisted of two departments—or counties—the Puy de Dôme and the Cantal, and that part of Haute Loire belongs also to Auvergne. The Cantal is less known than the Puy de Dôme. I was aware that few tales reach the outside world, and few travellers venture to that unknown region. There isn't much information available either. A prospective traveller, finding himself in the same abyss of ignorance, went to see Pierre Laval, who was an Auvergnat, and whose mother kept an hotel in Auvergne. That was before the last war. The future biographer of Laval will probably refer to the pre-war Laval as the good Laval, and to the one after the armistice of 1940 as the bad Laval. Anyway, the prospective traveller asked the good Laval for information on Auvergne. Laval thought for a while, then said: "Don't go to my mother—there are flies." And with that bit of useful information the traveller set out for Auvergne. I was in the same boat but with a vengeance: I didn't even know where Laval's mother's hotel had been.

I knew a certain number of Auvergnats in Paris, a town to which the Auvergnat refers as the second capital of Auvergne—Clermont, of course, being the first. They are mostly publicans and are in the wine and coal business. They make money in Paris. They work hard, are frugal in their habits and don't spend easily. They think that information about their native country has the value of cash:

thus not much is vouchsafed. But I did know, which very
likely they didn't know, that in the Tertiary Age there
existed in Auvergne little horses with three fingers—so said
at least a book I had read on Auvergne. An enthralling
picture.

Before I left Souillac I imagined Auvergne, and myself in
Auvergne, as follows: a jungle in the middle of London,
with snakes hanging from creeper-clad trees, lions roaring
and showing their yellow fangs, a rhinoceros ready to
charge, a buffalo doubling back on my track, and all the
time I can see on the other side of the palisade the 38 bus
on its way to Victoria Station. For once my fancy didn't
let me down altogether. Auvergne is a world apart, and if
one steps into it one is separated from France and the rest
of the west, as in my imagined jungle. But the palisade of
one's will keeps one in; for it can be left easily, France
remaining tantalisingly at one's elbow.

The Auvergnat is supposed to be endowed with the
characteristics of the Scotsman. I was, however, to find out
that the Frenchman observes his Auvergnat more shrewdly
than the Englishman his Scot. One thing certainly those
highlanders have in common: the Auvergnat has roughly
the same opinion of the French as the Scot has of the
English.

I knew that Auvergne had been the stronghold of feudal-
ism; of the Routiers; of Capitaine Merle of the Wars of
Religion; and that Cardinal de Richelieu, not trusting his
Auvergnat nobles, had the fortified castles demolished;
and with that meagre knowledge I said goodbye to
Souillac.

Souillac took a poor view of my journey. I was told I
would catch the cold of my life, wouldn't find an hotel fit
for humans, I would be cheated, and boredom coupled
with utter despair would soon drive me back. They said all

I would see were dead craters, red cattle and monsters in concrete, namely hydro-electric dams. No foie gras, no game of poker, and when the snow melts it rains incessantly. They saw I was determined to go, so they suddenly declared that Souillac was the gateway to Auvergne.

"Let me explain to you what Auvergne is like," said a commercial traveller who was passing through the town. "One winter night I arrived in a little town in the Cantal. It was bitterly cold, I wanted to stay the night, I went to the only hotel, it was dirty but I was tired. I asked the proprietress, a fat, red-faced woman, for a room. She said she had no rooms to let. 'What about that one?' I asked, opening a door. You see, you must never give in to them. The room was empty and there were two beds. She said she couldn't let it because I was alone. The room was usually let to four workmen at a time: two slept in each bed. 'Do you always let it to four workmen?' I asked. 'Always, except when the sous-préfet comes. He has the room alone.'" The traveller laughed. "You see the point, don't you? As I was neither the four workmen nor the sous-préfet I couldn't get that room for the night."

I didn't enjoy the story. He also told me that if one goes to an inn it is no good and serves no useful purpose to try to find out about the food. "*Vous aurez ce qu'il y aura,*" is the answer if the innkeeper bothers to answer at all.

"Don't go," chanted Souillac, and I was made a present of a bottle of marc. It was thought that I might be unable to find a drink in Auvergne. Some were of the opinion that I was pulling their legs, and was going back to Paris or London. Monsieur Lavergne, as president of the Syndicat d'Initiatives, had already written to his colleague in Aurillac, heralding my coming and asking him to help me during my journey as much as possible. Betz saw me to the bus which was to take me to St. Denis. The bus, a homely affair, arrived, I got in, the bus left and I felt as if I had climbed over the palisade. It was stuffy in the bus, and when we reached Martel I told the driver I was thirsty and in need of a drink. We both got out and drank wine while the other passengers waited patiently for us to return. Martel is a pleasant town, and I found the wine cheaper than at Souillac. At St. Denis I had to wait about two hours for the auto-rail. I took luncheon in the station restaurant where the food was surprisingly good.

In the station restaurant I met a little man with a rucksack beside him. He was middle-aged, shrunken and vaguely connected with Fleet Street. He was with a grey-haired, large, vivacious woman. Her travel accoutrement was in his rucksack. She opened it once or twice. That rucksack betrayed eloquently enough their intimacy; but that didn't satisfy the little man. Though ours was only a station encounter, though I wasn't particularly interested in their relationship, he couldn't allow the opportunity to lapse without acquainting me with the fact that beside the rucksack they shared the same bed too. His wasn't the voice of boastfulness: it was of gratitude. Good luck had brought her into his life: let all and sundry know.

"She is wonderful," he said when she left the buffet for a moment. "I mean my friend," he added, afraid lest I might, notwithstanding that we were alone, think he was referring to somebody else. She came back, they held hands, the auto-rail arrived, he put the rucksack on his back, and they travelled with me as far as St. Cère. There they got out and walked off arm-in-arm. They moved in step, which wasn't easy for him: she had long legs.

The English tourist is often hurt and not a little pained by the number of oaks he sees in the Lot. He doesn't mind poplars but has the feeling that oaks should grow in England alone. With walnut trees he is more tolerant—but only just. Now the oaks began to fall away. The auto-rail followed the course of some river or other in the opposite direction, since the rivers of south-western France come from Auvergne. There are many rivers in that part of the world, and it was difficult to guess, without having recourse to a map, whether it was the Dordogne, or the Cère, or the Jordanne, and the river or rivers I saw played their customary trick on me. There would be but a trickling rivulet, I would imagine the auto-rail was approaching the source of the river: then the auto-rail would rock through a tunnel, and on the other side of the tunnel I would meet the river again, fat and wide. Beside the tunnel there certainly was a hydro-electric dam. One never knows where one stands with the rivers near the border of the Cantal. Often some of the turbined water would disappear in an underground tunnel, reach a factory, do some work, then the industrious water would join the river lower down.

In my coach sat an old woman in the company of a young girl. She was pretty, slim, fair, and her left hand was a stump. She ate a banana, the stump pressing the banana against her breast, leaving her one hand free for the pleasure of conversation. She was gloriously unaware of her deformity. She was gay, pleasing to the eye, and in a little while I forgot the stump. She and the old woman alighted at a small station, and, as it happens, so inexplicably, an elderly peasant got in and his right hand was only a stump. However, he wore a sock on the stump. The peasant sat down not far from me. He was crying. He waved the stump in deep despair, his lone hand wiped the tears, and now and then it hid the eyes because the tears flowed too copiously. Perhaps there were too many for one hand to cope with them alone. Nobody took much notice of him. He shook his head, the stump waved and tear followed tear.

Was he, I wondered, crying for a lost favourite cow or a beloved sheep? I perceived on our arrival at Aurillac that the peasant was drunk, which, one must admit, didn't eliminate the cow or the sheep.

As the train stopped at Aurillac I noticed a change at once. There were no electric trains, the smoke of steam engines canopied the approaches. I didn't mind that. In spite of the speed and excellence of electric trains on the Hendaye and Toulouse lines, a train means hardly a train to me without the puffing engine in front. Those fast, silent electric trains give the impression that they hurry from place to place somehow under false pretences. I had reached my self-created jungle.

I searched for a porter but found none. I asked a passing railway official where I could find a porter. "Not at Aurillac," he said. "No porter would earn his living here. We are in Auvergne." And, as if to illustrate his point, a sweating peasant went by with a weighty trunk on his back. The station was lively, peasants abounded, but nobody seemed either happy or wishing to be so. The air was cooler than at Souillac. A long row of trucks stood on a side line. The lowing of the cattle in the trucks was louder than the snorting of the engine. I felt a stranger and could easily have believed I had left France. People were in a hurry: the leisurely gait of the Souillagais was far behind me.

I got into a small bus, a bus belonging to the *service de ville*. I was the sole passenger notwithstanding the low fare. The bus drove down a wide street. It should be said in favour of Aurillac that whichever way one looks one sees green hills. In the distance were the mountains covered with snow. It was the twenty-ninth of May. Little, unattractive shops flanked the street, we circled round the main square, and the bus stopped on this bank of the Jordanne at the Hôtel St. Pierre, recommended to me by a Souillagais who had once ventured as far as Aurillac. I entered a dark carpetless hall; the furniture was heavy and ugly.

Behind the desk sat an elderly woman in black, her nose flat, her cheeks ruddy: the peasant woman who had taken to business. She spoke in a loud voice, a voice brooking no contradiction. Later her son appeared, more suave, though underneath as hard as she. There was also the daughter-in-law, pretending to dress in accordance with the latest rules of *Elle*. Next morning in her working get-up she looked like any peasant girl. The grandchild—the dark hall wasn't without a grandchild—stood near the desk and shrieked. Parents and grandmother listened to it with pride. I couldn't ask for a room till the grandchild had decided to stop shrieking. Besides, if I had asked before, nobody would have answered me, as the child wasn't to be interrupted. The old woman said there was a room and turned her back on me. I begged her to listen to me for another minute. Luckily the child was taking a short rest, so I told her I should like to get in touch with the president of the Syndicat d'Initiatives. I said that not so much because I was in a hurry, but because if I saw the man to whom Monsieur Lavergne had written about me, I might not feel completely cast out. She told me the president was away, and wasn't for the time being interested in the Syndicat.

"He received a letter concerning me," I said, nearly adding: "Oh, what am I to do now? I am lost, lost."

"There is a secretary," she said grudgingly. "He's an accountant. You may telephone him."

"I don't think I'd know how to telephone here."

The grandchild started up, so we all had to wait. Eventually she got hold of the accountant, who said he would look in on me after luncheon the next day.

I suppose the best manner to acquaint oneself with a

strange town is to sit in the main square outside a café. I sat down in the square and looked round. I didn't have to look for long before I saw I was in a sparkless provincial town, dedicated to the Prefecture, the Palais de Justice and the prison. The Palais de Justice was on my left and the prison next door to it. A woman with a parcel was loitering before the prison. She was a young woman and waited patiently. At last the door opened a little, she ran to it, before she could reach it the door banged, and she walked away, her head bowed, the parcel under her arm. Almost in front of me was an imposing building, which was, needless to say, the Gendarmerie Nationale. The chestnuts of the square were in bloom, and there was a superb public lavatory.

At a table beside me three men quarrelled. Two quarrelled in patois, one in French. Coaches came and went, cattle were whisked through in closed lorries. A woman crossed the square followed by a dog, two men stood in the middle of the road chatting, a bus hooted, the men took no notice, the three men at the next table had stopped quarrelling and were laughing loudly. A closed lorry passed the café: six searching eyes stared through the bars, the eyes of three bullocks. They weren't, so I fancied, looking for the Palais de Justice or the Gendarmerie Nationale: they were trying to locate the slaughter house, of which, however, no other bullock could have given them a description. There is nothing like sitting outside a café in a strange town and letting one's imagination go free. The Aurillac dogs were out in number, better fed and better kept dogs than the dogs of the Quercy. I managed to understand better the snatches of the local patois I overheard than the patois spoken at Souillac. But it didn't make me feel more at home.

Everybody seemed satisfied with himself: I was to observe

that throughout my trip. An old story comes to mind. God on the eighth day created the Auvergnat. He offered him the most delectable regions of the world. He could choose for his home whichever he wanted. He said he wanted to live in the Puy de Dôme, which is sheer anachronism. On the eighth day the Puy de Dôme was still called Basse Auvergne. It was named Puy de Dôme only in the reign of Louis XIV. But let that pass. "No, my dear Auvergnat," said God, "you can't go there. The volcanoes are still in eruption. Auvergne is burning."

"I can wait," said the Auvergnat, and ever since then, so the tale implies, the entire world has to admire the good taste and patience of the Auvergnat.

A woman pushed a pram to the terrace of the café. It was a wide pram: three small ugly faces were side by side in the pram. Triplets; and a man rose from a table, and the woman said: "Here is your uncle. Uncle is going to kiss every one of you." The triplets howled; nevertheless, uncle kissed every one of them. With one child it would obviously have been less noisy. Triplets have their disadvantages. Another man approached: he was hailed as another uncle: I paid and went back to the hotel, where I dined in a gloomy dining-room which could easily have been a waiting-room in Liverpool Street Station. A local guide book refers to the enchanting panelling of that dining-room. After dinner I walked through the old town. Most of the old buildings were restored at the beginning of the century or in the nineteen-twenties, including the House of the Consul, which now is the home of the Caisse d'Épargne. Only the sculptures on the door in the rue de la Conte remain unspoiled. Near the Jordanne a fair was in progress; but no circus.

The circuses which tour provincial France are irresistible to me. A few days before their arrival posters cover the

walls of towns and villages. If one trusted the posters one
would believe that performing pythons would dance with
beautiful maidens from the East, tigers would swallow
elephants, and Red Indians would jump on the backs of at
least two hundred caparisoned black horses. At times, like
expensive shops with only one dazzling item in the window, alone the head of a monstrous, angry animal is displayed on the poster, to make one understand that a horde
of such animals is waiting threateningly in the circus. Then
the circus arrives and a poor, starved, mangy lion gazes
dolefully from the covered wagon. There are exceptions
such as the Cirque Amar and the Cirque Pinder, entire
towns on the move, bringing along all the enthusiast could
wish for.

Generally those small circuses call themselves either
Grand Cirque de Paris or Grand Cirque de Marseilles.
That is a convention promising as little as an election
speech. Therefore I was intrigued the year before at Souillac when a circus introduced itself as plain Cirque de
Limoges. To be but a circus of Limoges was a sign of
shattering modesty. I went to it on the first night, and had
to admit that the modesty was well founded. The circus
owned only one animal, a monkey which wasn't fit enough
to perform that night, though for a small additional fee
the monkey could be peeped at in his cage. Some of the
peasant children, who had come from the plateau with their
parents, went to visit the monkey and came back impressed. One said he believed the monkey was dead. His
father called him an idiot, and said he was pretentious too.

A trumpet was blown, and a fat woman in tights
appeared. Slowly she found her way to the trapeze,
climbed up, sat on the trapeze and picked her nose. Now
and then she started swinging energetically, and just when
one expected something to happen, she stopped swinging,

the trapeze became motionless again and her finger took to her nostrils.

Down in the arena things were looking up. The clown and the circus manager had come in. They told each other smutty stories for half an hour. At intervals they remembered the woman on the trapeze, pointed at her, she would swing a bit, then, their duty done, manager and clown went on with their dirty jokes. The peasants and their wives listened attentively; if the children's interest flagged they were prodded by their parents. A story about an artificially fed grandmother went down exceptionally well, and mothers told the children to remember every word of it, and under no condition to forget it. The tale was easy to remember.

"What," asked the manager, "is your grandmother given now that she has to be artificially fed?"

"A huge beetroot," said the clown; and on long winter evenings the children recited the joke to their parents.

"And now, ladies and gentlemen," said the manager, looking up remorsefully at the forgotten woman on the trapeze, "Mademoiselle Odette, the great trapeze artist, will sell you nougat of Montelimar, and I hope you will buy large quantitites, for she is a great artist. Come down, mademoiselle: everybody is waiting for you."

Mademoiselle slid down swiftly, the clown opened a battered suitcase, took out the nougat and mademoiselle got busy. Manager and clown, forgetting to announce the interval, rushed off to the nearest café, where they drank for a solid forty minutes. On their return to the circus they announced the interval was over. They were wise people: this time they sent mademoiselle round with the nougat in the middle of a joke. They knew it would be fruitless to wait till the end. They spun out the joke, mademoiselle sold, and when she had stopped selling she left, and the

joke came to an end. The manager produced a pack of dirty
cards, he and the clown amused themselves—the audience
saw and understood nothing. The clown said: "It was a five
of hearts." The manager said: "If you say so it certainly
was." And mademoiselle walked through the ring in a
raincoat. That was the signal for clown and manager to
pocket the cards, and they rushed off to the café. The
audience waited a bit longer, then as nothing happened it
left; and just in time because the clown rushed back, like
one who had forgotten an important matter, and turned
the lights out.

The following afternoon the circus of Limoges had a
cinema matinée. The poster announced a film starring Rintintin, the talking dog. Some of us might still remember
Rintintin from the days of the silent films.

But, alas, there was no circus at Aurillac, and even the
posters of the last visiting circus had been defaced by the
electioneering slogans of the Communist Party. "Americans back to America," seemed to be their favourite. The
inhabitants of Aurillac go early to bed. I looked into a few
empty cafés, saw a few lorry drivers trying to keep awake,
then returned to the hotel. My room was gloomy, the light
weak and I didn't feel like sleeping.

I read some guide and travel books, which had been given
to me or I had picked up. Many of them were written and
edited purely to carry advertisements of local factories,
shops, and the produce of the district. They all boosted the
Cantal and boasted of the Cantal. Some of them, as I was
to discover, were blithely inaccurate; but what does that
matter to the editor if he receives a fat sum from a factory
of galoshes or from an expensive restaurant? The other
irritating aspect of those books, with the superb exception
of the *Guide Michelin*, which is accurate, concise, intelligent
and to the point, is the authors' solemn intention to write

what they consider beautiful prose. The authors are frequently present or past presidents of the Syndicat, or the chamber of commerce, or a late mayor or deputy, or even a senator.

The first which I read gave a description of the Cantal. It began with this gem: " . . . *les larges vallées glaciaires creusées par les eaux vives des torrents où foisonne la truite.*" It would have been more to the point, and certainly less pretentious, if the writer had stated that the rivers and lakes of the Cantal were well stocked with trout. At any rate I had already noticed that I entered a trout belt. Every restaurant displayed trout on its bill of fare—the Hôtel St. Pierre's trout being the most expensive.

A man snored in the room on the left, to the right a bed groaned with lovers, and groaned most of the night. At dawn the commercial travellers began to rise. Alarm clocks went off, cars were started up, but the one who snored, snored on happily. Then more alarm clocks went, and I was wakened again. I was angry, and when angry I pick up my missiles if needs be in the past. Once, irritated by a pompous Dane, I said to him: "Thank God Nelson burnt your awful ships." It didn't distress him; and now with the noise of those who were leaving, and the placid snores of the one who was staying behind, I exclaimed: "Well done, Caesar, I should have done the same to that awful Auvergnat." Of course I was referring to Vercingetorix, the pride of Auvergne. Auvergne is proud of every Auvergnat, and every Auvergnat is proud of Auvergne. For the Auvergnat even geology is on its knee to admire him. There is something in that: Auvergne was the first in France; but the Vosges and Brittany had also appeared in the Primary Age. Auvergne took little notice of them.

I fell asleep only to be brought back by the sound of bells. I went to the window: in the bright early sunshine a

herd of red cattle was hurrying along the waterfront, a man
with a stick and a busybody dog in their wake. The beasts
were red—the red cattle of Salers, and the guide books
refer to that breed as the famous cattle with the mahogany
cloak. One guide book said the cows of Salers remained
unshakably faithful to the high traditions of their forbears, which meant they were good milch cows.

It was a warm morning, the sky was blue above the green
hills, and the sun picked out the trees, the river and the
lorries coming across the bridge. On top of a hill the sun
shone on a clump of trees. Those trees are called the
Twenty Trees, and the people of Aurillac take great pride
in them, as if there were twenty trees nowhere else. So I
counted them: only twelve; but I kept that to myself. I
walked down to the Pont Rouge. The old houses came
down to meet the river, which then fell gay and foaming
over a waterfall, the waterfall hurling it under the bridge.
A number of women scrubbed and washed linen in the
open, the smell of Eau de Javel was pungent. The snow-
capped mountains were astonishingly near, and a man said
to me it would rain in the afternoon, adding there would
be no summer this year.

"But we Auvergnats don't mind," he said. "We are a
hardy race."

I had breakfast outside a café near the bridge. Cattle and
sheep were arriving in lorries; in an open lorry travelled
three calves. Two stood and swayed: one sat quietly in the
middle. Our eyes met and I felt convinced that calf knew.
Yes, it knew, and it was no good pretending it didn't. It
knew and was grimly satisfied. Its eyes declared it couldn't
be otherwise, it didn't matter, it was the right solution;
in fact, those eyes seemed to encourage me to eat more veal.

A forenoon followed with not much to do. The *Guide
Michelin* admits that Aurillac has little to offer except a

museum devoted to the history and the geology of the Cantal. In a narrow street a fat postman told me the contents of the museum had been moved to the military barracks. The town was full of peasants. Two types can be distinguished with ease. The dark, almost Saracen, the blond or ginger, blatantly nordic. Roughly speaking, those are the two types of the Cantal. The fair, according to my experience, predominate. In buses, coaches and trains I amused myself by counting the colour of eyes and hair of the passengers, and the nordic won. The peasants favour large moustaches: some old women vie with them. The peasants often ride to town on saddled cart-horses which they don't tie up but walk about the town while bent on their errands.

I went to see the Cathedral of Nôtre-Dame des Neiges. Before the Revolution it was the chapel of the Convent of the Cordeliers, belonging to the Order of St. Francis. The chapel is believed to have been built in 1222. Tradition has it that St. Anthony of Padua, on one of his Apostolic journeys, preached in the chapel. In 1339 a fine church and convent took the place of the wooden chapel; in 1569 the Protestants set fire to the church, but the walls remained. The church was rebuilt. In 1666 lightning hit the bell, in 1792 the church became the Temple of Reason. In 1802 Aurillac was divided into two parishes, and from then on the church was known as Nôtre-Dame des Neiges in memory of the victory against the Protestants on 5th August 1581. (Dates, one might say, just dates, Yes, dates—but the history of France in a nutshell.)

The cathedral was restored several times. The Gothic sacristy I admired. It used to be the refectory of the Cordeliers. The black Virgin in the second chapel is a copy of the Virgin of Puy.

I stayed in the cathedral for a while, walked about slowly,

reached a copy of Velasquez's Christ, and an old woman approached me. She stopped and asked me whether I was a stranger. She wore a cavalry moustache. I said I was.

"This," she said, "is a church."

I thanked her. She sighed, repeated it was a church and disappeared in the shadows.

I strolled about the town for the rest of the morning. Aurillac is an imposing coach centre. If one studies the names of towns and villages of the coaches' itinerary one receives a geographic education on the Cantal. I could have worked out a journey round the Cantal at random. After a bit of aimless walking I found myself again in the big square. I sat down in front of the café of the night before. Two gendarmes hustled a young man through the prison door, three dogs fought languidly, and my watch said it was time to lunch, since the secretary of the Syndicat would be calling on me at one-fifteen.

The panelled dining-room was full. The guests weren't from Aurillac: they were businessmen, cattle dealers and lawyers. They all called for specialities of the Cantal, which delighted the red-faced, elderly woman; for specialities are invariably expensive; and if one feels like it one may call anything a speciality. That was no fault of hers: she was the proprietress of a restaurant.

Next to the leader writer and the editor of a left-wing weekly, to the restaurant keeper alone is vouchsafed an unassailable belief in himself. If he gives one mediocre food he none the less is convinced that one never ate better before. If one complains he knows one is a dunderhead who understands nothing of food. Modesty swept past him before he was conceived: the client's purse is blessed if it is put at his disposal: the very fact that the client is permitted to eat within his precincts should fill the client with joy and gratitude. Restaurant keepers are all the same, the only difference being that one gives better food than the other. That bursting red-faced woman was a symbol of the entire profession. She hovered over those who ordered specialities. I, because I had ordered the menu and drank but half a bottle of rosé, was proudly ignored.

At the next table were lunching two Parisian lawyers. They both wore horn-rimmed spectacles and their cheeks were pale. One of them, short and thin, shook his head at intervals, saying: "Auvergne". He would stare at his plate, shake his head again and say: "Auvergne."

"It gave us Pierre Laval," said his companion.

"Auvergne," he said.

"Blaise Pascal," said his companion.

"Auvergne."

"And Lafayette. You must admit Lafayette was born in Auvergne."

"And," his companion said, becoming suddenly vivacious, "Lafayette jumped into history on horseback. That's all he did. Got on a big horse, spurred it and jumped on its back into history." He glared at his plate. "Auvergne," he said, and shook his head.

The red-cheeked woman came up to tell me the secretary of the Syndicat was waiting for me. I ate fast; nevertheless, I found leisure to observe a man devouring trout at a nearby table. He was the novelist's dream; for it was shamefully easy to describe him. He had eyes like a frog, a mouth like a frog, sat like a frog, in brief looked like a frog. If he had suddenly jumped on a trapeze I should have said a frog on a trapeze. He had finished eating, rose and put on his raincoat. I said to myself: a frog in a raincoat. He walked out of the restaurant like a frog. In the door he dropped his dispatch case. A frog, I was convinced, would have done the same.

The secretary was waiting for me in the hall. He wore

spectacles and his handshake was unenthusiastic. He was a
man without enthusiasm. I asked him if he had received
the letter announcing my arrival. He said he hadn't. The
Syndicat functioned only as from the fifteenth of June, and
before that date no letter was opened. I smiled and nodded
as though to imply that it was perfectly understandable
that letters shouldn't be read before the fifteenth of June.
If they were, calamity was bound to follow. I explained to
him that I had a travel book of sorts in mind, a travel book
about his Auvergne. He wasn't interested. He listened to
me politely, absent-mindedly.

"The elections," he said when I had finished, "are driving
me mad. I am a member of the M.R.P., but the candidates
take up too much of my time. Of course I want my party
to win, but I have my own chores to attend to, don't you
agree? A man can't dedicate himself completely to his
party, can he? One has one's own business too. Which
party will win? What do you think?"

"The General," I said, chiefly to annoy him.

"No," he said complacently. "You foreigners don't
understand our politics."

I didn't remind him that it wasn't I who had volunteered
a forecast. I asked him whether he could help me in any
manner, that is give me information about the country,
places worth visiting and so on. We were standing and he
seemed impatient to be gone.

"The peasants," he said, "make a lot of money. But we
are a very shrewd race. Take the Auvergnat who goes to
Paris. I knew one who started without a sou, and now has a
flourishing café in the Boulevard Sebastopol. Do you know
the Boulevard Sebastopol? *Très commerçant.*"

I said I knew it but Paris at the moment was no worry of
mine. Perhaps he would tell me of Auvergnats nearer home.

"You should have gone off with our candidates this

morning," he said. "It is too late." He looked at his watch. "I must go back to the office. But come with me as far as the Syndicat. I have some books which I can lend you."

We went to his office, which was in the big square, a kiosk, damp and dirty, as nobody had been to it for a long time. He gave me two books on Auvergne, both uncut. I remembered that the chief engineer of the Ponts et Chaussées of Souillac had spoken to me of an hotel near the hydro-electric dam of Saint-Étienne-de-Cantalès. The secretary said yes, that was a good hotel. I asked him to ring it up. He did so. He said to the hotel-keeper a person wanted to spend a few days at his hotel. He didn't bother to add that the person wanted to see as much as possible of the countryside since that person intended to write about it. I was to find out in the course of my stay in Auvergne that while the Auvergnats scream for tourists and can't understand why other regions are more favoured by them, they will do mighty little to further their wish. They sit back and praise themselves and their land, which on second thoughts is admirable.

The door of the kiosk was open, a fat man came in, asked the secretary whether the season had begun. The secretary told him it hadn't: he was busy with the person over there, and in a minute he would lock the place up. He spoke in an irritated voice, as he had no wish to waste more of his time. But the fat man was in no hurry: he walked about, took down books, looked at the posters, examined leaflets, whistled loudly, and when it seemed to him he had seen all he wanted to see he left the kiosk.

"People like that drive me mad," said the secretary. "They think the whole world belongs to them."

"Which, you must admit, is an elevating thought."

He didn't agree with me. He was kind enough to trace

me an itinerary. I stuck to it while I was in the Cantal. He gave me a list of hotels. I went to them, and if they were bad and expensive, it was simply because there was nothing better. I thanked him profusely.

"As I know, the whole world doesn't belong to me . . ." he said, shook hands with me and was glad to get away.

He told me before we parted that I should, when looking at Auvergne, think of the Routiers, and the fear and devastation they brought with them. I said I had the Routiers continuously in mind. It might have shocked him if I had added that in an exotic, perverted fashion I had a sneaking regard for the Routiers, which, I suppose, is a form of rebellion against the indexed, numbered and planned existence one is commanded to lead nowadays.

The Treaty of Calais on 24th October 1360 gave the Quercy to the King of England, thus Auvergne became a frontier province. The Companies, therefore, had no difficulty in attacking Auvergne with ease, notwithstanding that King Henry undertook, in accordance with the Treaty, to abolish them. The Routiers, who formed those Companies, were of many nationalities, though were led usually by Englishmen. They loved adventure, had no desire to go home, fighting was their sport, they despised honest routine, and they went about devastating the land, practising rape on a large scale, spoiling churches, holding the rich to ransom and even forcing frightened priests to say Mass for them on Sundays. They were led by knights, noblemen, bastards of great houses; now and then also by vagabonds, varlets, peasants and brigands.

The burghers of towns had reason to fear them most. They held them to ransom; the ransom money was frequently above their means. If they came to a town not only had the town to pay in florins, but often had to provide them with cloth, barrels of wine, furs, spices, fish and, if the Routiers needed them, with workmen too. The Companies were well organised. Next to the Routiers, who were the soldiers, came blacksmiths, saddlers, butchers, physicians and clerks who worked out the figures of ransom money and how much the town should pay. Their wives and mistresses lived with them, and the English Routiers, God bless them, sent for their English wives. And the wives came out from England, joined their husbands, and thus fortified the husbands sallied forth to burn, pillage and rape. In the excellent organisation of the Companies there was room for merchants, that is for capable men who sold the looted goods. As they were pushed out of Burgundy and Beaujolais, so they concentrated more and more on Languedoc and Auvergne. They threatened the papal city of Avignon, and in February 1361 they promised to evacuate Pont-Saint-Esprit and go to Italy to fight the Visconti with the Pope's money. Some went, Sir John Hawkwood was one of them, but the big majority stayed behind and continued to harass France. Pope Urban V excommunicated them. It took nearly another century to rid France of those men who refused, as we should say, to settle down.

Before I left Souillac the charming English wife of a Scottish doctor said all she knew of Auvergne was that there were some caves near Clermont in which the English used to hide from the Auvergnats. I assured her it was the other way round.

When I parted from the secretary I reminded myself one can't have it both ways. One either complains of the presence of too many tourists, or, if one goes off the beaten track, complains of the lack of interest evinced. I returned to the hotel and asked for my bill. The woman with the red cheeks and flat nose charged me more for my room than I had the habit of paying in Paris for a far better room. The same applied to the second-rate food, and eighteen per cent. was added as tip. I inquired why she had chosen to charge me with eighteen per cent. She said six per cent. was the *taxe de séjour*. I pointed out that in a restaurant no *taxe de séjour* was charged anywhere else in France. Perhaps for the room but surely not for, say, an omelette or a glass of beer. Do people who come to drink or lunch pay *taxe de séjour*? Her fat red fingers drummed on the desk, all she vouchsafed was her flat-nosed profile, and when I had reached the end of my well-knit, irrefutable argument she said thank you, turned to the maid, and they chatted near the carpetless staircase till, knowing I was beaten, I left.

I couldn't help reflecting that such unpleasant surprises come mostly one's way in mournful, boring, small towns that have little to offer. During my countless travels and sojourns in France I was, to use the vernacular, stung generally in towns where the finest building was either the Préfecture or the Gendarmerie Nationale. Elsewhere, I can truly say, practically never. Perhaps in those sad towns they overcharge one because they know one will not come back again. I went to a café near the bridge. I showed the bill to the proprietor. On such occasions one believes erroneously that sympathy can be found at every street corner. The proprietor was, however, sympathetic. He explained that the St. Pierre was known for its high prices; and then he charged me double for my drink.

I had a couple of hours to while away before the coach I was to take would leave for Laroquebrou, the nearest stop to Saint-Étienne. In front of the café was the statue of General Delzons, a soldier of the Emperor. He fell in battle during the retreat from Moscow.

Chapelain, in his poem of the Pucelle, refers thus to Aurillac:

> *Nourissons d'Aurillac où, dans ce siécle encor,*
> *Le fond d'un lac séché brille des veines d'or.*

Which is quite wrong; for ever since the Tertiary Age there is no lake at Aurillac. The history of Aurillac is remarkable, but the majority of the towns of Auvergne are, as it were, tied to history. One easily feels that one should recount the entire history of France if one is interested in the past of the towns of Auvergne; and without their past the towns would have little to say.

In the tenth century Saint Géraud built an abbey, and the town of Aurillac grew up round the abbey. The monks of St. Géraud educated a young shepherd called Gerbert, a boy of great gifts. They sent him, once his rudimentary education was finished—they gave him all the knowledge they themselves had—to Spain, where he studied at the Arab universities. To Gerbert is attributed the transplanting of the Arab figures into the western world. His renown reached the ears of the Emperor, who made him the tutor of his son. Gerbert was raised to the Papacy in the year 999, and was the first French Pope, under the name of Sylvester II. He was the Pope of the Year One Thousand, the Year of the Great Fear. (I am haunted by a sentence which my memory can't place. I found it in a French book, dealing either with history or architecture. I found it a long time ago. The sentence alone stays with me, but stays indelibly. It said: the great fear of the Year One Thousand was but an excuse to cover the beautiful land of France with the white mantle of her Gothic churches.) Pope Sylvester died in 1003.

The town began to prosper in the days of St. Géraud. Previously it was a small hamlet surrounded by dense forests. The monks of St. Géraud cultivated the rich land and cleared the forests. St. Géraud died in the Lot, some say in 909, others in 920. As time progressed the burghers of Aurillac became rich, and they fought for their rights, as they called it, against the abbot, notwithstanding that his predecessors had created the town and their wealth. But that is progress. They fought with their consuls at their head. The number of the consuls was six, each of them elected for one year.

During the Hundred Years' Wars the English occupied several fortified castles in the vicinity, and frequently tried to take the town. They were unsuccessful. In 1429 the consuls gave the King of France two hundred men who, led by Joan of Arc, took their share in the victory of Orleans. Charles VII came to Aurillac in 1434 to thank the town for the help it had given him.

The Wars of Religion brought misery, violence and death to Aurillac. The opposing parties were described by André Imberdis, an Auvergnat historian, in this manner: "The Calvinists were conspicuous by their sober enthusiasm and austere solemnity. They prayed together morning and evening. The old French gaiety, good humour and recklessness remained with the Catholics, who went to battle in accordance with the traditions of chivalry; everything for God, love and battle." Which shows that Roundheads and Cavaliers don't belong exclusively to the British Isles.

Thanks to a traitor inside the town the Huguenots occupied Aurillac on 5th September 1569. Many of the inhabitants were massacred, priests and monks were buried alive, churches and convents burned down; for the Huguenots were of the opinion that one had to get rid of the cotes in order to get at the pigeons. On 10th October 1570, a few months after the Treaty of St. Germain, the Huguenots withdrew, but the wealth of the town was gone, all works of art destroyed, the three convents of the Carmes, the Cordeliers and du Buis in ruin, and at the end of the occupation the original population of eight thousand numbered but six thousand seven hundred and twenty-four souls.

The revenge of the Catholics on the Night of St. Bartholo-mew consisted of making eighty Protestants jump from the Tower of Colonhe, and they broke their necks on the stones of the road beneath the tower. In 1575 the Hugue-nots made an attempt to retake the town. They came in the night, but the bells pealed on their own, and the enemy was repulsed. The final attempt was made on the night of 4th August 1581, and this is what the chronicler Labrohea wrote:

"The miraculous and merciful Mary, our patroness, made a miracle for us by lighting up our town with a light as bright as only the sun could give, and thus the light of that miraculous day woke up all the poor inhabitants . . . daylight before its time, given by the grace of Mary, was only inside the town, and only for Catholics, and it was very dark outside the town so as to confuse the heretics . . . the Holy Virgin appeared to some who saw her on top of the Gate of Aurinques, holding in her arms her beloved son Jesus."

The Protestants climbed the ramparts on ladders, a bugler reached the parapet, blew a fanfare and then shouted: "The town is taken." One of the defenders fired a shot at him. In the morning the bugle was found at the foot of the ramparts. The Protestants were repulsed, chased and never attacked Aurillac again.

There was plenty of cruelty displayed on both sides. The Huguenots excelled, however, with leaders like the Capi-taine Merle and François de Beaumont, baron des Adrets. Those leaders were in a sense the sour heirs of the Routiers. To their rapacity and cruelty was added bigotry. The Routiers seem far more likable.

Prosperity came back to Aurillac in the epoch of Col-bert, who founded the lace industry. During the Revolu-tion the guillotine worked industriously in Aurillac. One day one hundred and sixty citizens were arrested, suspected of counter-revolutionary impulses. They were sent to Paris; luckily the convoy arrived after the 9th Thermidor; one citizen alone was beheaded, the others were allowed to go home. Nowadays Aurillac is proud of its manufacture of umbrellas, which, so the guide and travel books unanimously declare, are in brisk demand owing to the climate.

"Do you know," said the café-keeper who had observed that I was reading a history of Auvergne, "that Vercingetorix was an Auvergnat? He defeated the Romans."

I said I knew. It would have been a waste of words to tell him that Vercingetorix was defeated by the Romans in the end. The ears of the Auvergnats are deaf to such facts. I could have told him, which wouldn't have amused him, that I was intimately acquainted with Vercingetorix, an acquaintance that went back to my childhood; for as a little boy I saw a film about him. It was during the First World War, and the film was, to say the least, naïve. Childhood memories stick to one, are polished daily by their own vividness, and if I hear the name of Vercingetorix there appears before me a man wearing a helmet with two horns, a vast moustache, his head is bowed, he is in chains, and at the time I thought he resembled an ox. That was probably due to the horns. The film moved fast, and before he could lift his bowed horns a man wrapped in a bath towel materialised, and gesticulated wildly. The man was baldheaded. Suddenly they both disappeared, and their place was taken by a train coming out of the tunnel at Monte Carlo station. I was afterwards told that I had seen Caesar with his captive Vercingetorix.

"We the Auvergnats," said the café-keeper, "always win our battles."

Chapter Four

SAINT-ÉTIENNE AND THE DAMS

THERE are certain words and phrases which fire the imagination. I knew a man who affirmed his heart thumped deliriously whenever he heard anybody say Western Approaches. There are those who swoon when one recites to them: *"Je suis le seul, le veuf, l'inconsolé . . ."*; and they can't be blamed for it. From my first visit to Souillac onward I was invariably impressed by the words *les grands barrages du Cantal*, especially as I hadn't seen any of the hydro-electric dams. I imagined them as a stately row of bastions, rising, probably, higher than hills and mountains. Later I learned, but only from hearsay, that they were a mass of concrete and each dam held, as it were, a lake on its back. One of the big dams of the Cantal is called Aigle, and I couldn't help picturing a weighty eagle of the Emperor, wings spread from one mountain-top to the other.

During my third stay at Souillac I had a short story in mind. In that short story I wanted to describe the inundation of a river, a river resembling strikingly the Dordogne which at the moment was high, and brushwood raced along its angry surface. I vaguely understood there were dams at different spots and they held the river under control up to a point. I went to see the engineer of the Ponts et Chaussées, and asked him questions based on sheer ignorance. What I needed, I explained, for my story was a leaking dam. I wanted to write of a leaking dam that would let the river sweep along villages, uproot trees, bring misery and devastation to thousands, and the good and the bad would drown together. It was February, a dead month;

why shouldn't everybody perish with that month? Dams, the engineer explained, didn't leak like that, though now and then they leaked a little. Leakages were called foxes in the argot of engineers.

"Foxes?" I asked.

"Foxes."

"I'd have some difficulty in springing foxes of that sort on the English short-story reader."

"They are known as foxes. But if you are interested in dams, you should go and see *les grands barrages du Cantal*."

My heart thumped; and now I was in a small, noisy bus on my way to the dam of Saint-Étienne.

The fertility of the countryside through which we rattled was impressive. Arthur Young would have praised it crisply. Pastures, fields and more pastures, and the one word that came to mind was fat. The grass was fat, the soil was certainly fat, and the cattle, after the extended winter's fast, were becoming fat. And in the bus were fat peasants and fat peasant women. It appears to me that in Auvergne men and women are either fat or thin. There seems to be no medium. Our bus was loaded with fat people; everybody shouted, not with annoyance just to hear his voice better. The bus was crowded, but in France buses are either crowded or empty. The bus stopped in a village, a woman got out, another woman was expecting her at the halt. They kissed, chatted, kissed again, the bus waited, they talked seriously, unhurriedly, kissed, shook hands, the woman who had alighted got back into the bus, and we went on. The bus stopped in the next village, they all got out, a thin man with a black moustache and beady eyes remained alone behind. He eyed me for a while, then came and sat beside me. He smelt of sweat.

"Where are you going, monsieur?" he asked.

"To Saint-Étienne."

"Are you an engineer?"

"I'm not."

"Anything to do with electricity?"

"I'm afraid not."

"Then what are you going to do up there?"

"Look around."

"Well," he said, "I wouldn't bother to look around Saint-Étienne."

"Where would you like me to look around?" I asked.

"Clermont: very nice shops there, and the cinema every evening."

"But the grand barrages," I said.

"The what?"

"Nothing," I said, and we sat in silence. In a little while he muttered something about having to get off soon, and left me. He must have found me an unenlightened fool. The old belief that country folk appreciate the country is as good a fallacy as any. The cinema at Clermont means more than the calm, serene lake at Saint-Étienne. And who should blame them? They see enough of the country, which in time of drought or too much rain is more of a harsh enemy than a background for bucolic pleasures and frolic.

A woman got in. She was fat, and her double chin spread from ear to ear. She was happy. She sat engulfed in her happiness, and told the driver in a happy voice that she was going to Laroquebrou; and when we reached Laroquebrou, which is the nearest stop to Saint-Étienne, I alighted before her. Happy people are in no hurry. The church of Laroquebrou is Gothic and of the fourteenth century; the bridge was already there in the thirteenth. Laroquebrou had possessed seven chapels; now only the hospital's chapel remains. It dates back to 1294. I went inside and saw a statue of St. Sebastian in painted stone. It is of the fourteenth century. I found it impressive, but later on the Mise-au-Tombeau at Salers pushed all other painted stone statues from my memory. That is, alas, the price one pays for perfection. (One becomes, for instance, perhaps too critical of Romanesque churches after a visit to the church of Saint-Amand-de-Coly in the Dordogne.)

I had been told that towards seven o'clock a bus would take the children of Saint-Étienne back from school, and I could go with them in that bus. They were, so to speak, the children of the Électricité de France, that is the children of the employees at the dam and the transmission station. I walked as far as the river Cère, and I said to myself it would be difficult after my trip to Auvergne to find again such bewitching, small, clear and fast rivers, adorned with enchanting waterfalls; and so many rivers at that. They belong to fairy tales, to children's story books, their beauty and freshness almost irritating because one knows that one had pictured them like that before disappointment, sorrow and the ups and downs of existence had knocked such images out of one's mind. A grey-haired man came up to me and asked whether I was the person who wanted to go to the Hôtel de Pradel at Saint-Étienne. I said I was the person, and he said he was the manager of the hotel, and would drive me to Saint-Étienne in his car.

He was a helpful, amiable man, and, as it turned out, an excellent hotel-keeper, his wife a truly good cook, their daughter charming, and it is nice that for a change I can praise an hotel unequivocally. It was the best hotel I found in the Cantal. He told me I would never believe that the lake was the the result of the building of the dam, and not of nature at its kindliest. As I have spent a good slice of my childhood near Lake Como, lakes are for me what an early love affair is for the amorous sentimentalist. Lakes should be filled with tears, weeping willows should caress them,

9

and if I think of lakes I am ready to forgive Lamartine his sloppy poetry. And the lake at Saint-Étienne turned out to be the lake I was thirsting for. It is a lake for lovers, for the harpsichord, for full moons in spite of the rain that kept me company on its shore, for those who believe in balanced sadness, unriotous gaiety and in the sheer pleasure of meditation and thinking not too harshly of themselves.

The car stopped outside the hotel, which is beside the lake, and instead of going to look at my room I hurried down to the lake. The water rippled peacefully, drowsily, reflecting the green foliage of the trees. It was powdered with rain, and I could have rubbed my cheek against it. It looked as though a sharp carving-knife had cut the contours; at any rate the lake seemed happy within its confines. It is narrow where it faces the hotel, one sees little of it, yet it is about eight miles in length, and a thirty miles' walk to go round it. Promontories abound, trees and bushes flourish, and all one hears is the silence of the water and the cuckoo in the distance. Rain and the cuckoo remained with me during my stay, both, frankly, monotonous but for the lake. It is difficult to believe that ten years ago there had been a valley and the shores were the top of a chain of hills. The bushes were green and yellow, the pastures of a darker green. During the dry summer of 1949, when there wasn't enough water for the turbines of the dam, the water was let out of the lake. I asked the hotel manager what it had looked like while the valley, so to speak, returned. He said it wasn't a delectable sight. The houses, which were in the valley and on the sides of the hills, had crumbled almost completely, a few walls alone remaining. The rest was mud—dead mud.

The hotel belongs to the Électricité de France, which took it over with the dam when the private company that owned Saint-Étienne was nationalised in 1945. It is a white building with rust-coloured roof and shutters. They seemed to be the official colours of the Électricité de France, as all buildings belonging to it at Saint-Étienne were white with rust-coloured roofs and shutters. The man who had decided on those colours must have hailed from the Basses Pyrénées. I had a simple, comfortable room, a good bed, and my room was next to that of an old man, the only other guest in the hotel. I never found out what the old man was doing and why he had come to Saint-Étienne. He was, probably, employed like everybody else in the neighbourhood by the Électricité de France. On the ground floor was a long room serving as dining-room and bar for the unmarried employees of the Électricité de France. They lunched and dined in there, were noisy and ate heavily, taking care that they got their money's worth. The dining-room of the hotel guests was upstairs.

Outside the hotel was a terrace with some chairs. I would go out to have a drink but wouldn't sit down because of the ceaseless rain. If I took with me, say, a Ricard, I had but to hold out my glass, and the rain filled it with the necessary quantity of water, and I didn't have to say 'when.' To stand on the terrace in the rain and gaze at the lake was a pastime from which it was difficult to tear myself away. The road was between terrace and lake: there was little traffic. The smoke of rare trains on the other side of the lake seemed to be the sole connection with a world from which I had gone. The cuckoo was an early riser.

Near the hotel were the buildings which housed the staff and workmen of the Électricité de France. It came into existence in 1945, when the light and power companies were nationalised all over France. Though it is a vast corporation with headquarters in Paris, it has a certain flexibility and isn't averse to private capital: in fact, at the time of writing, it launched a loan for more hydro-electric dams. For the success of the loan it had to rely on the aid of the high finance of France. I couldn't help reaching the conclusion that in several respects France is more suitable for a corporate state than Britain. Both the Électricité de France and the S.N.C.F. (the French Railways) are proof that corporations can work smoothly and efficiently in France. Those whom they employ take pride in their work, there is keen competition among different departments and regions, and a sense of esprit de corps; and the wish to work in order to advance hasn't disappeared with the advent of nationalisation.

One explanation comes to mind which, like most explanations, is probably too simple—the explanation might be Versailles, that is the centralisation of the power and the majesty of the state, as thought out by Cardinal Richelieu and put into practice by Louis XIV, whom I could easily imagine as the chief of the Électricité de France or of the S.N.C.F.—possibly the chief of both of them— and he could have taken the Banque de France in his royal stride too. It should be added that in the Électricité de France the thirst for promotion struck me as similar to that in the French Army, and the Électricité de France is organised on similar lines, namely officers, N.C.O.'s and men. An engineer at the dam of Saint-Étienne, speaking of an electrician who was getting married, said to me: "Of course he will never get higher than such and such a post." So the distinction is perhaps more strict than in the army.

As an illustration of the pride those corporations' employees have in their work, I can't but evoke a dreary Sunday in Gourdon. I was returning from the hospital, and only a small train with timeworn carriages was going to Souillac. It was a cloudy day without the hope even of rain. A thick, middle-aged man sat with me in the compartment—an employee of the S.N.C.F. We chatted and he spoke to me of the new rails on the Paris–Hendaye line, rails that would make it possible for the express to travel faster through the Landes. No lover could have spoken with more emotion of a fresh love, and when he held up both hands to show me the kind of rails they were—I know nothing of rails—it was like a doting parent showing the height of his baby. And when at Saint-Étienne they spoke of high-tension cables, it was with the same intensity of love. If a river was mentioned they said oh yes, that one has millions of kilowatts, or it wasn't much of a river from their point of view. Water was either turbined or not yet turbined: otherwise water had no meaning.

Fine rain was falling on the first evening. It came down inexhaustibly, and there was no reason why it should ever stop. I stood outside the hotel, but then the rain sent me indoors, where I was surrounded by electricity. In that new village which had come into being on account of the dam one talks and thinks of electricity alone. In the hotel I was the sole person unconnected with electricity. For the employees of dam and transmission station, who lunched and dined in the hotel regularly, the lake was a matter of sufficient water or not enough water; the weather was gauged the same way. Now and then some stranger arrived, but his errand was connected with electricity. Once, while I was there, a Swiss turned up: he had come to study at the hydro-electric plant. Two English engineers studied there before him.

When on the first morning no hot water came out of the hot-water tap in my bedroom and I mentioned that to the hotel manager, instead of saying, as it is said so often in French hotels, the boiler would immediately be stoked up or other guests had had too many baths, in short the usual excuses, he said there must be something wrong with the thermostat, and he would telephone the Électricité de

France to send somebody to attend to it. (Incidentally, I hadn't let the water run long enough.) On the other side of the lake grazed a few red cows; their bells gave an echo to the silence, but cows and bells were interlopers in that condensed world of electricity. The repetitive cuckoo, on the other hand, sounded as if it was sitting on top of a pylon.

On my first evening I walked down to the dam. The transmission station is on a hill overlooking the dam. A man, naturally employed by the Électricité de France, stood near the dam and explained to me that the dam and the station had nothing to do with each other.

"But look," I said, "at those cables going up to the station."

"I am speaking from the administrative angle," said the man, more astonished by my attitude than by my ignorance.

Darkness was falling on the placid lake, its water lapping the concrete wall. A road crosses on the top of the dam; a car swished past, the headlights picked out the trees on the other side of the dam. I stopped and looked down. The concrete wall fell almost gracefully towards the river below me, first in a straight line, then curving above the turbine room. Along the wall three huge concrete fins ran down to the edge, or rather end, of the turbine room. To the right of the turbine room the water used by the turbines—*eau turbiné*—falls into the river. Months of unremitting rain had filled the lake, and brought the water on the other side—that is the side which held back the lake—nearly to the top of the concrete wall. The sluice gates were closed, but my informant explained they would soon have to let some of the water out of the lake. The night was flat down, the lights shone through the windows of the turbine room, and I went back to the hotel. In an ordinary French village I should have had to pick my way in the darkness: here, however, there was a street light at short intervals. I met nobody on the road. That didn't seem to worry the street lamps. They knew that at Saint-Étienne they weren't a luxury.

In the night a fast wind was blowing; it banged doors, and brought more rain in its wake, rain which came to stay. Before my window in the morning was the rain-powdered lake, clouds toppled over each other, and the thought of a clear sky was unimaginable. A man in a raincoat cycled along the road: a little later a lorry of the Électricité de France churned up the pools, and silence followed. The rain was absorbed noiselessly by the rising lake. I went down to the dam, took another look at the man-made precipice, and on my return to the hotel was introduced by the manager to the chief engineer of the dam, a man resembling a lovable teddy bear. He hailed from Lorraine, was kind, intelligent, and a friendship sprang up between us under false pretences; for, so the hotel manager had explained to him, I had come to Saint-Étienne to write about hydro-electric dams. The chief engineer said he was delighted, though not surprised: there were few subjects more enthralling than hydro-electric dams, and if I was an electric engineer . . . I murmured I wasn't. He would, the chief engineer went on, show me round the dam, but not today: one of the turbines had been cleaned and wouldn't start working till next day, and it wouldn't do to show round a visitor with only one of them turning. He said that as one says: don't come today for dinner; come tomorrow: the food will be better.

"Since you are interested in dams," he said to me, "I will drive you to Chastang this afternoon. Chastang is in the Corrèze. A big dam is being built there, much bigger than this one. It is nearing completion. It will have the two most powerful turbines in France. I am certain they will impress you. Chastang is about twenty-five miles away."

He came to fetch me at two o'clock, and as we drove off
I tried to explain to him that he was taking a complete tyro
along who didn't even know how the telephone worked.
He thought erroneously that I said this deprecatingly. We
left Saint-Étienne behind, a waterfall came into view, and
the Cère, which for a brief instant was the Cère again, fell
over a concrete wall and was now the lake of Nèpes. That
waterfall, explained the chief engineer, would soon be
turning a turbine. "The turbined water of Saint-Étienne
and the excess water . . ." he was saying. I didn't quite
understand him. I did, however, appreciate that if the water
of the lake of Saint-Étienne were let out uncontrolled,
Laroquebrou and the land round it would be totally
inundated. A pretty village was perched on the hillside,
grey-brown against the hill, the slate roofs navy blue against
the grey sky. We drove through Laroquebrou, took a
steep road ; the Cère was deep down to our left, the water
clear in spite of the fast falling rain, and he stopped the
car.

"Here," he said, "the water, that is some of it, goes into
a tunnel, and through that tunnel to a factory seven miles
away. In normal times the entire river flows through that
tunnel. But in this rainy weather there is plenty left for
the old river-bed too." The rain had become vehement.

"I take it," I said, "that electricity is very cheap round
here."

"Oh no," he said; "you see, there are dry summers, and
then we must use coal, which is very expensive."

"But this year," I said, "one could surely make it
cheaper."

"It doesn't work like that."

Of course, I reflected, it doesn't work like that. Somehow or other it is the consumer's task not to benefit. A
rainy year like this one puts nerves on edge, caters for

rheumatism and frays tempers, yet to give a little pecuniary sunshine by lowering the price of electricity is out of the question: it would be sheer pampering. Moreover, next year it might be dry. I was reminded of a sage but sour friend of mine in Souillac. Last year, or perhaps the year before, I overheard somebody saying to him the coming harvest would be a bumper harvest.

"I'm not moved," said my friend. "All my life I heard of bumper harvests, yet I never ate cheap bread."

The chief engineer informed me he would soon be leaving Saint-Étienne to take over at Chastang. He was going every day to the dam as the skipper of a big liner goes to the shipyard in order to become acquainted with the ship he would be commanding after the launching. Chastang meant promotion to him. He then talked of his career and said he had served at sea during the First World War.

"Did you ever sail with the Royal Navy?" I asked.

"Only against it," he smiled. "As I am from Lorraine I was in the Imperial Navy."

We reached the Dordogne, drove alongside the river. "The dam," he said, and there was the monster before us. First we went up to the top of the dam, We got out of the car, and walked on the concrete. Words such as bedlam and hell are often bandied about; but on top of the dam I understood what bedlam meant: hell was still to come. There were workmen by the hundred, some hanging on the side on rope ladders, and apparently not one of them falling, though the drop was nine hundred feet; others were moving about with cables and wires ; trucks backed, dropped their load and left, riveting and hammering made as much noise as the winches; and whichever way I looked there were notices of *Danger de Mort*, and again and again *Danger de Mort*; and the din was deafening. On top of the hill to the right, as if hanging in mid-air, was the cement-mixing installation. On the hills were pylons, shaped like evil stars, holding cables on which moved prehistoric creatures with screeching that would send one panting into the nearest cave. There was noise of steel, of cranes and all sorts of engines, sparks flew, chains made the din of numberless dropping anchors, and in a silly fashion I was reminded of a French film in which the crippled intellectual husband limps through such a racket with his beautiful wife. Half naked, broad-shouldered workmen loll about with splendid torsos, and one of the workmen, who whistles of course, catches the wife's eye, whistles louder, and her eyes then feast off the torso—and the tragedy for the husband begins. But the workmen on top of Chastang were mostly slim men, and the rain induced none of them to show his torso.

"Seven hundred thousand tons of concrete here," shouted the chief engineer.

"Are there many accidents?" I shouted. That was foremost in my mind.

"Only seven this year," he shouted and jumped aside to let a lorry pass. "They usually fall down the side, but one of them, believe it or believe it not, killed himself simply with a lamp."

"I believe it," I shouted. I was ready to believe anything.

"Another got electrocuted just over there," he shouted, but I didn't look in the direction he pointed.

A lorry backed towards me. I took a step backwards and knocked against a chain. On the chain hung a board, and on the board was written: *Danger de Mort*. I felt I had my share. I approached the parapet. A workman swung over the parapet, holding the end of a steel rope in one hand, climbed down a rope-ladder, and sitting in mid-air he took a lighter from his pocket and relighted his cigarette, which had already been between his lips when he swung over the parapet. I left the parapet only to jump from the chain of an advancing crane. At last the chief engineer took me to his car: I thought my ordeal was over. I was wrong, and it was now my turn to find out what hell meant.

We drove down and went inside the dam, where we were encompassed by concrete; it was an empire of concrete with no life and no resurrection left: the concrete alone ruled. Dark and grey it surrounded me, weighed me down. The noise was that of a nightmare. I looked at the men working inside that soulless world, a world which frightened me, which boded no good. The men, visibly, didn't care. They hung on chains, sat in cranes, stood on scaffolding, tested engines, and one near me, holding a soldering lamp, whistled a tune all about love. The noise left them un-scathed, and I clearly perceived they didn't much mind whether they were inside or outside the monster. Ad-mittedly that mass of concrete was a triumph in many respects: to me in many ways it was a sad surrender.

The chief engineer and I walked on planks and scaffold-ings, and underneath us were workmen in deep chasms—probably whistling too. By now the chief engineer was aware of my ignorance, though not of my fear.

One of the two turbines was already in place; in fact, it would start turning in a month's time, and that would be, as it were, the opening of the dam of Chastang. The chief engineer took me to see it. It was of 135,000 horse-power, and the second turbine would be of the same strength. They would be the biggest turbines in hydro-electric France. The Americans, apparently, have more powerful turbines, but for me 135,000 horse-power sufficed. And, interestingly enough, they sufficed also for the chief engineer. When we came out he said he was worried a bit about the turbines: 135,000 horse-power wasn't to be taken lightly. At Saint-Étienne the turbines were a mere 45,000 horse-power each. What, he couldn't help asking himself, would happen if something went wrong with such a huge engine and they couldn't close either the sluices or the valves, and water would continue to pour in with the turbine out of control?

"But," he added, "I won't allow myself to get frightened."

"Why," I asked, "do they build such vast turbines? Forgive me for this silly question. I am completely ignorant in such matters."

"Man's lack of modesty," he said, and in my ignorance I should have given the same answer.

He took me to see the transformers and I hoped I should now be allowed to leave the monster. No: I had to mount endless stairs of concrete, with walls and ceilings of concrete round me and above me; and oh, I sighed, give me the steps at Roc-Amadour. The lifts weren't functioning yet; nevertheless, he insisted on my seeing the control room. I was duly impressed by the thousands of electric wires, switches and gadgets, and compared it to that of a battleship, said it was wonderful, how clever the electricians were, and then I was permitted to go. On the side of the dam an enormous steel contraption was being dismantled by whistling workmen. We returned to the top, and I looked at the trees and yellow bushes of the valley, which would be inundated, that is, drowned, in time. Again I was wrong. The valley and the hillside would be cleared before the water was let in. The water would come slowly, would rise slowly; and there would be no headlong rush to please my imagination.

"But," said the chief engineer, "it happens inexplicably that for no reason whatever the water suddenly rises quicker than was calculated."

It gave me a little joy to think that the elements had a

small say, their bondage notwithstanding, in their own affairs.

"I know what you're thinking," said the chief engineer. "Man has gone too far." He, however, was thinking of the turbines.

We parted from the monster and drove to Argentat, a quiet old town with an old bridge, the old houses reflected in the Dordogne; and I had the frightening notion that, without warning, seven hundred thousand tons of concrete would appear and crush the old houses and old bridge. We went to a café. Four men were playing belotte, a fat fellow talked to the patronne of the price of steak. My fear still clung to me. The chief engineer explained to me that with the dams, the rivers would be better controlled, inundations could be eliminated, there would be more water during the dry seasons; in brief the dams were a benefit to mankind. He had a good word for the concrete too: it behaved well in water.

Outside in the narrow street a pretty, dark-haired woman was hurrying with a big parcel under her arm. Another pretty, dark-haired woman hailed her.

"I come," said the first, "from a funeral. Wonderful food and so much of it too. I am taking this," she slapped the parcel, "to the children. So much was left over."

"Was there foie gras?" asked the second.

"Plenty of it. I must run." She turned back from a small distance. "They say the woman died of four cancers." She turned back again. "Four," she called.

"In a dam," the chief engineer was saying, "it is as on board a ship. The chief engineer is the captain, and he is responsible if anything goes wrong. He has his officers and crew." He smiled with professional pride. "For me to take over Chastang is as if I were given the command of the Queen Mary."

"But the Queen Mary," I said, "only rides the waves."

On our way back to Saint-Étienne I said it was a pity I knew not one of the technical expressions of the lingo of dams. He said a man had come to visit the dam at Saint-Étienne, and had a dictionary in five languages of all technical words used in connection with hydro-electric dams: English, French, German, Spanish and Portuguese. The man who possessed that treasure was a Pakistani engineer. "Nonetheless," said the chief engineer, "we couldn't understand each other. He couldn't converse in ordinary French."

That cheered me up a little; and after a rainy night came a rainy morning. The cuckoo was at it again. The chief engineer came to fetch me in the rain and took me to the dam of Saint-Étienne: I was to see the monster in civilised garb. On the top of the dam, where I had gazed the day before at the lake on one side, and the precipice on the other, was an almost concealed short staircase. We went down, reached a door on which was the familiar notice *Danger de Mort*. He unlocked the door, and took me inside. There was the sound of engines and trickling water, we were engulfed by concrete, but it was comparatively urban. We were taken down in a lift, and I was impressed by the telephone in the lift. We got out in a passage, the walls were painted yellow; there was some woodwork, the doors were of wood; lamps of somewhat modern, though homely, design were everywhere, and it was akin to being in a modern office building modelled on the inside of a ship. We went to the control room: it was impressive. It was explained to me that this here—whatever it was—controlled one turbine, that there controlled the other, over there was the control of the sluices, and to the left was the control of the valves, this showed the volume of water coming in, that dealt with electricity; and all the time telephone bells were ringing. The chief engineer took me to his office, where he asked me what I wished to see. I said I wished to see the spot where the water came in. That made him laugh; for the water comes in deep down because one has to reckon with the water of the lake being low in dry seasons; furthermore, the spot I desired to see was, of course, under water. He showed me on a chart how the water entered the dam. It reminded me of the tunnel of a ship through which goes the propeller shaft, with the difference that the propeller of a dam, that is the valve, is at this end of the tunnel.

He took me down in a lift to the turbine room: he wanted to be present when the cleaned turbine started to turn. I witnessed it and for my uninitiated eyes it was a case of whirling; on the other hand, the deafening noise when the water was let in brought back my trip to Chastang.

I was rather surprised to hear that Saint-Étienne was built during the occupation. For Chastang to reach the same state of urbanity it would take another three years. Chastang would have no wood—only concrete and steel. It was still raining outside, so I was in no hurry to leave. I wasn't thinking of the weight of the lake against the concrete. We chatted, I brought a fresh mind to the problems of hydro-electric dams, and must have talked nonsense eighteen to the dozen. The chief engineer was interested in the result of the nationalisation of electricity in England. I said electricity was more expensive. He said he had thought that would be the result. The morning went by; I sat in the office or nosed about in the control room, and towards noon the turbine, which had been put into action and was doing its stuff, began to generate electricity. Before I took leave I inquired how far was electricity taken from Saint-Étienne.

"All over France," was the answer, "and at times it travels on the pylons to Spain, Italy, Switzerland and

Germany. In a dry spring when the snow melts in Switzerland, the Swiss send us electricity, and when it freezes in Switzerland we send them electricity. You must look at it as you look at railway lines which connect western European countries.''

I heard him tell his assistant that the sluice gates should be opened in the evening to let some of the water out of the lake, because due to the rain the water had risen almost to the parapet of the dam. I learned the lake normally held 130,000,000 cubic metres of water, and each turbine generated 30,000 kilowatts of electricity.

Once one enters the world of electricity there seems no escape. At luncheon the hotel manager told me the chief engineer of the transmission plant wanted me to visit it in the afternoon. That invitation, as I was to discover, was based partly on hospitality and on the desire to be helpful, but mainly on professional jealousy. Little love was lost between dam and the transmission station. For the staff of the dam the plant was a species of parasite which lived on them. For the staff of the plant the dam was a colourless humdrum bit of wall which would have been of no use if not put to better purpose by the plant. In the pouring rain which hid the other side of the narrow lake, I went to the plant, brushed past many signs of *Danger de Mort* and was shown round by an enthusiastic young engineer. Anything I asked was answered on paper, that is he made some complicated calculation or drew a diagram, and I understood neither of them. I would smile and tried to look like an eastern sage: my smile, however, was too polite. In fact, it gave me away.

"You aren't,'' he asked, "a scientist?''

"Not really,'' I said.

In the same fashion as my Souillagais peasant was impressed by the tractor, I was affected by the young

A Valley of the Dordogne

Cantal: the Hydro-Electric Dam of Saint-Étienne

A Virgin of Auvergne: Nôtre-Dame de Saint-Flour

engineer telephoning on a high-tension cable. Apparently it is out of the reach of most mortals. He explained to me that the whole electric system of France worked together, and if one switched on a light, say, in Paris—to switch on a light would have been frowned at by him: one asks for electricity—the current might come from a power plant worked by coal in the north of France, or from a dam in the Alps; and as he talked the immense natural wealth of France became almost tangible. Electricity can come from the Rhine or the Rhone, and when in early summer the rivers of the Massif Central are low, the melting snow of the Alps and the Pyrénées comes into play. I thought of the exquisite excitement in store for me when I would ask for electricity the next time—that is when I would switch on a light—would the light inside the bulb originate from the Dordogne, the snow of the Pic du Midi or from a grim factory near the Belgian frontier? Needless to add that when I asked for electricity that evening I simply switched on the light and noticed a fly on the wall.

I caught sight of a poster on the wall. The young engineer was still talking, but the poster absorbed my attention. A man on the poster stood with an electric cable in his hand; zig-zagging lightning was rising from his waist upwards; and he was gazing down at it with the solemnity the situation asked for. I interrupted the young engineer to ask him whether such accidents were frequent.

"If they are stupid enough," he said. He shook his head. "One can't play about with electricity. Fools always think they know better."

That evening before dinner I drank in the hotel with the engineers of the dam and of the transmission plant, listened to their technical conversation, observed the rivalry between the two services, and began to wonder whether I should, in the near future, become an electricity bore. I could, I sensed, bring enthusiasm to it, but no understanding and that is the main attribute of a bore. The chief engineer of the transmission plant found out that I wrote books. He said he wrote too, though only for his pleasure. He sent one of his assistants back to his house, who returned shortly after with an elegantly bound typescript. The chief engineer inscribed it to me and the next morning he was disappointed to hear that I hadn't read it yet. The title was *En Plantant des Pylônes*, and I did read it from beginning to end. It took me a month or so. It is the story of the chief engineer while he moved about in Auvergne planting, as he put it, pylons. It can't be recommended for reading even on long winter evenings when the television set is out of order; and certainly not to readers who don't believe in television. For me, however, it had a sort of charm: the chief engineer didn't care for the manners of the Auvergnats; he was a Parisian and never forgot it. The book is mostly about food—in fact, a record of good and bad meals. He got lyrical over a *petit salé* he had eaten in a village of the Haute Loire, or vitriolic about a *tripou* he was given in the Cantal. His pen would linger over an *omelette aux truffes*, and it would become nasty and slanderous when the steak wasn't tender. The pylons were but an anaemic shadow in the dining-rooms and kitchens he had frequented.

"I don't want it published," he explained. "It might cause controversy."

In some kitchen, I thought to myself, and thanked him for his present.

After dinner I walked to the dam. One of the two sluice gates was open and the darkness was filled with the din of rushing and falling water. I looked over the side of the dam. The water poured down between two of the fins, then hurled itself into the lake of Nèpes. It was as if a

thousand white virgins, all tied together, were leaping joy-
fully to death. The rising foam was like a cloud, and above
it rose a mist of foam. The lights of the turbine room
picked out the foam: the virgins were blushing. On the
edge of foam and spray stood a tree; in the darkness that
tree resembled a lecherous, bearded old man who had come
to gloat over the fall of the white virgins. Virgin pushed
virgin and on they leaped. Somewhere in the Acroceraun-
ian Mountains Arethusa surely cried.

I stood there for a long time and didn't want to go. It is
exciting food for thought why certain memories and
moments are gilded by what one believes in retrospect to
be beauty, while other memories and moments die. With
me there remain images which I savour whenever I gaze at
them: the ringing of the Angelus in the square at Ana-
capri, a cock-pheasant walking through a clump of daffodils
in East Suffolk, the sun lighting up Hylarion in Cyprus,
and a few more; for not too many are given to me. Among
those images the water pouring down the concrete wall of
the dam in the crepuscule has now taken its deserved place.

It is worthy of thought too that the monster in concrete
took its place beside the Annunciation of Leonardo; but
let it be added it was the monster for once at the disposal
of the elements. Nevertheless, a monster.

As the water fell with the night falling on top of it, I
knew I had seen all I wanted to see of hydro-electric dams,
and electricity I sent back into the vast sea of ignorance
and astonishment within me.

It rained till the morning of my departure. If I hadn't
seen a map I wouldn't have been able to place north and
south. On the last day the sun popped out, as if he were a
Jack-in-the-Box. For a few seconds the lake was marked by
little golden spots. Then the box closed. A commercial
traveller had arrived the night before. He was lean, and

given to personal questions. He asked me, for instance, whether I believed in birth control, parliamentary government, the elimination of the unfit and American cars. I answered at random. By then he was aware that I wrote books, I had a son, a dog, no car and liked my steak underdone.

"Do you write all the time?" he asked.

"God forbid. There are days and weeks when I don't feel like working at all."

"I am like you," he said. "There are mornings when I awake and don't feel inspired at all. On such days I don't go near my clients. But there are mornings when I am choc-a-bloc with energy, and simply throw myself on my clients. The same thing, you know."

"What do you sell?" I asked.

"Artificial manure," he replied.

The planter of pylons drove me to Aurillac, and I was sorry to leave the best hotel I had found in the Cantal.

Chapter Five

SALERS

THE big square of Aurillac depressed me once more, I saw
the triplets again, and saw two gendarmes hustling a young
man through the prison door. I sat outside a café, and
a dyed blonde with red fingernails and redder lips sat at
the next table. With her sat an ordinary peasant girl in
black, the only red about her was the weather-exposed
colour of her cheeks. When they parted they embraced
affectionately. I had gathered from their conversation that
they were sisters. One had gone to Paris, the other stayed
behind on the farm, and the parting of ways and their
different mode of life had made no difference in their
relationship. It is a great and admirable quality of the
French that there are no snobbisms or pretensions attached
to one member of a family leading, according to rural
standards, a glamorous existence in Paris while the other
tills the soil. One can often notice in Paris restaurants
men, dressed in all the trappings of the successful Parisian
business man, lunching an old peasant woman, ordering her
an expensive meal, doting on her, glancing proudly at the
other clients, and he is a proud, happy man; for he has
brought along his mother. A friend of mine, driving on a
road of France, saw a Cadillac pull up abruptly, an elegant
man jump out, rush up to a shrivelled little peasant, and
they kissed and embraced.

The bus for Salers left from behind the prison of Aurillac. It was a tiny bus, the rain had given way to brazenly
hot sunshine, the bus was already crowded, and it was
smelly. The windows were closed. A young abbé and I

wanted to open the window. The other passengers, most of them elderly women in black, attacked us at once. The heat and the smell hadn't sweetened my temper; moreover, they sounded too righteous and too aggressive. I said to the loudest and smelliest of the women: "Do you want us to asphyxiate?"

"Asphyxiate?" she shouted. "I had an operation only three months ago. I don't want another operation just because you open the window."

The abbé pointed out gently to her that if the windows were opened on one side there would be no draught. It was useless. The bus was with her, and she was explaining for her partisans' benefit the dangers another operation would involve. In front of me sat a peasant who smelt of hospital refuse, including thrown-away medicine bottles. The bus left, it became hotter, and the bus bumped along the road, with hills, woods, pastures, and here and there a waterfall accompanying it. The bus shook through Saint-Cernin, a small town overlooking the Doire. Between the shoulders of two women in black I caught sight of a Romanesque church. A shoulder moved: the church was gone. A third woman in black blew her nose into her palm. We crossed a viaduct to the sound of a waterfall. The countryside was almost painfully green, the hills rose, and so did the road, rather imperceptibly. Red cattle grazed in the fields.

We stopped in a small village. I went to the bistro to take air and have a drink. An old woman with a red face and white hair served me. I had noticed in the bus a somewhat finicky woman, probably a Belgian, and she had held her handkerchief to her nose throughout the journey, for which she couldn't be truly blamed. Nevertheless, she wasn't likeable: she ostentatiously abhorred bad smells, and abhorred them in a genteel fashion. Now she tiptoed into the bistro, afraid that her shoes might be contaminated by the dust and the cigarette ends on the floor. She stopped before the counter, leaned over and whispered into the old woman's ear.

"What is it you want, ma fille?" the old woman asked loudly.

The woman put her hand before her mouth and whispered again.

"Oh, that," said the old woman. "Go out into the courtyard. Plenty of room out there."

The finicky woman blushed and didn't go out. According to the driver of the bus we should have left in five minutes. It turned out to be twenty minutes. He was a man who had gloriously escaped the rule of time. The road, when we left, twisted gently, as if afraid that the bus would turn over with its pungent load. The hills continued to rise unnoticeably, the fields were studded with the red cattle of Salers, the tinkle of their bells penetrating through the closed windows. A woman had a coughing fit; then I heard the bells again. Our progress could best be described by comparing it with a short story by Henry James. Too verbose here, one feels like saying; a bit obscure there, one admits; and what is he driving at with all those words and in so obscure a fashion? Suddenly, even before one has time to breathe, the story is driven home, one sees his point, one has reached the end, one is astonished, verbosity is forgotten, obscurity waved aside, for everything fits in perfectly. In a similar fashion, what with the twisting road and the gently rising hills, I suddenly perceived that we were high up, the hills had turned into mountains, their green plateaux moving towards the waiting snow.

Before us was the town of Salers, the houses of basalt and trachyte, black in winter, grey in summer. In his *Commentaries*

Caesar mentioned a black town he had seen in the distance in Gaul. The people of Salers like to think he was referring to their town; and for Caesar's sake I hope it was Salers. It wasn't. The bus entered the town and in a strange fashion I felt I had arrived, a feeling not every town is capable of giving. The bus stopped in the Grande Place, now named after Tyssandier-d'Escous, the man who in the last century had started the breed of Salers cattle. Incidentally, the herd book was closed only in 1930.

The square with its fountain and fifteenth- and sixteenth-century houses—one house alone is of a later period—is, what guide books would call, unique. The architectural style of the houses is a blend of Gothic and Rennaissance, but it is the colour and, one might say, personality of the stones which are the most impressive. After a winter of heavy snow and a spring of continuous rain the stones were just beginning to turn grey—some were still black. The hotel proprietor's daughter was waiting for me, and she took me to the hotel through narrow streets lined with old houses, the majority of them of the same stone, a few built as late as 1700, yet retaining the style of the town.

Of the hotel, alas, I can speak but sorrowfully. As the other hotel is of the same calibre, I needn't mention mine by name. Suffice to say Salers has no decent hotel, which is indeed a pity, since it is a great joy and experience to visit that town. Nevertheless, I shall, the hotels and their sanitation notwithstanding, not hesitate to go to Salers again.

I was taken to a room with four doors and two double beds. I was assured that I would sleep alone: the tourist season hadn't started yet. Of sanitation the hotel was mostly innocent: what there was could well have been left out. I dined alone in the dining-room, though it had enough long tables to accommodate a host of guests. On the chimneypiece stood a clock. It was the epitome of bad taste, belonging to the French Exhibition of 1867. It was of bronze, two bronze female figures held it, a cherub squirmed beneath the clock, but it should be added that it fitted in with the ghastly wallpaper. I thought while I ate a huge meal, which, in spite of the excellent quality of meat, vegetables and butter, had been cooked without the slightest trace of culinary imagination, that those who live in the lap of nature learn little from it in matters of taste. Taste, I suppose, is an acquired pastime of the leisurely minded. I admitted immediately that was a hasty and sweeping statement caused probably by the noise of the children in the hotel. For it was polluted with children, each of them shouting for six. Dogs and cats walked in and out: so did the children. The vista of four doors and two double beds had made me irritable and crotchety.

The large family of the hotel-keeper lived and ate in the kitchen, which was a sort of mart too. The smell in the kitchen was delicious. I was reminded of a story related by one of the engineers at Saint-Étienne. He had gone to some town or other in Auvergne, went to a restaurant, was given an indifferent meal consisting of omelette, escalope, chips and cheese—the sort of meal one gets in any restaurant anywhere in France. Two workmen came in, sat down at the next table and were served *tripou*, a regional dish which can be excellent. The engineer inquired why he hadn't been given the same. The answer was they thought that strangers liked only Parisian food. Probably the ample dull food I had been given was considered Parisian too. *Tripou* is made with the tripe of sheep.

I went to my room, where a solitary bulb tried unsuccessfully to pick out the revolting pattern of the wallpaper. I asked for a stronger light, and was given a tiny table lamp. That was understandable enough: those who don't read would find it more than adequate. It was useless to argue, so I didn't insist. There are times when all that is left to one is to pray for sleep. The sheets weren't inviting, and I had a good mind to pull my pyjamas over my suit; and I hated myself for grumbling. Why should small matters of no consequence put one in a bad mood? Before I could answer that I was already asleep. I woke up with sunshine gripping the room. I found the proprietor shaving in the kitchen, the children shrieked. That day I was served again with copious tasteless food. I must say drinks were surprisingly cheap. The day was Sunday and at noon the family sat down to something resembling a banquet in the kitchen. There were at least twenty of them. They shouted in patois, but weren't merry. Generally speaking the Auvergnat isn't merry. His sense of humour is of the sardonic variety. The discomfiture of others makes the pastures ring with laughter, drowning the tinkle of cowbells.

On Monday I was given for my last meal a juicy steak with which was served a cheese soufflé. My last night in the hotel hadn't been peaceful. The proprietor's son was a lorry driver. He drove cattle to markets, and cattle, to judge by his alarm bell, rise early at Salers. The alarm bell went at four-thirty, and then with lamentable swiftness the whole family rose. There was shouting and talking, doors banged, the lorry was driven to and fro in front of the house. The wooden staircase reverberated with heavy footsteps, as if everybody in the hotel wore hobnailed boots. There was such rushing down the stairs that I half expected to hear the *générale*; but the regiment stayed within the walls.

During my two days' stay in the hotel no notice was taken of me. They gave me a roof, beds, food, lighting of sorts—and all that because they had undertaken to do so. They were neither friendly nor unfriendly; I didn't exist

146

outside their strict duty. Not one member of the huge
family bothered to ask me whether I liked the town, had
slept well or was satisfied with the food. They didn't know
where I came from, which wasn't a case of lack of curiosity,
but of total lack of interest. Not one word or gesture was
vouchsafed me outside their appointed duty. Everybody
else in Salers was friendly and helpful. I must admit that I
retained a certain respect for the hotel-keeper and his
family. It was imposing to be so completely detached from
one's way of earning one's living. They had rooms, they
gave food, and with that hotel-keeping began and ended.
It wasn't laziness; it was the fruit of icy detachment. Even
their smiles were under control There was, however, one
fleeting contact between us. Before I left the mother said to
one of her many daughters: "Ask him, perhaps it's for
him."

The daughter showed me an airmail letter from Canada.
She explained they had received it a year ago. I said the name
on the envelope wasn't mine. "It's always like that," said
the daughter, and put the letter away.

The first morning I went to the Promenade de Barouze,
where spreads before one as fine a panorama as one could
wish for. The Promenade is shaded by trees but is in
patches burned by the sun, which that morning was hot,
making the countryside sparkle, as though it was getting
ready for an elegant party. The Promenade is surrounded
by what is left of the town walls. There the Protestants
climbed the ramparts on the 1st of February 1586, were
repulsed, and where they had been driven off a Cross was
erected. I gloated on the landscape. Beneath me through
the green meadows flowed streams towards the valleys of
the Maronne, the Rat and the Aspres. The mountain
slopes were covered with trees, their foliage thick and dark
in the sun. The plateaux were treeless, green pastures rose

slowly, delicately towards the distant snow. Behind them towered the Puy-Violent, but there is nothing violent about it. Sheep used to graze up there by the thousand, and the noise of their bleating floated into the town. In patois to bleat is *belant*, and *belant* in time turned into *violent*. I couldn't see the Puy-Mary because it was shrouded with mist. The fields of the valleys and the plateaux were divided by stone walls. I was vaguely reminded of North Wales—vaguely is the word. The red cattle sprinkled the green of the landscape. It was difficult to believe in the hot sun that six miles from Salers the road to Peyrol was closed because of snow.

When I left the Promenade I went along that road, reached a farm, and near the farm grazed a herd of red cattle, and red calves sat in a pen. The colour of that breed, the herd book of which closed so recently, is of the same red as Red Polls; in shape it looks very much like Welsh Black; their horns aren't yet standardised. The people of Salers, in fact the people of the entire Cantal, are proud of the breed. Raising of cattle, which is the biggest industry of the Cantal, is based on the Salers. Of their milk is made the cheese called Cantal, and speaking of that cheese it is as Cheddar used to be before the last war. The trouble with the Cantal cheese is that they don't let it mature enough, but if here and there one finds well-matured Cantal it is an excellent cheese.

As I stood looking at the cattle, listening to the bells on the red cows' collars, with the Chapel of Nôtre-Dame-de-Lorette on the other side of the road, and near to it the workhouse founded in 1537 by a local noble, I reminded myself that I had a date to keep, a date I wanted to be rid of. I gazed at the town, black turning into grey, the houses clustered together, the church tower like the bonnet of some huge nurse keeping the children near so that nothing should befall them ; it appeared to me that I was miles from Salers, though I was but a few hundred yards from it. But such small old towns, so compact and sticking out on a hill or a mountain-top, often give one that sort of optical illusion, and they seem pleased with the fast one they have pulled. The date I had was the result of a few minutes' conversation I had had in a café the evening before.

In Salers there are sixteen cafés. For a population of six hundred that isn't a mean figure. One of the cafés in the Grande Place is called the Café d'Agriculture. Its door was closed. I tried it, but it wouldn't open. As I turned away a woman flew to the door from the depth of the café; then the door burst open. She had scorching black eyes that leaped into flame at the sight of a prospective client. "Come in, monsieur," she said in a voice that brooked no nonsense. I meekly went in. In the far corner sat a man, a black hat on his head, his hair grey under the hat, the moustache black, the eyes red-rimmed. He ate like a rat: quickly, furtively. In the other corner sat a girl in front of a sewing machine. She had blonde hair, blue eyes and a rosy complexion, and any English advertisement of an English face-cream could have been proud of her.

The woman engaged me in conversation. Wasn't Salers the most beautiful town in the world? Wasn't the cattle of Salers the finest cattle in the world? I said yes, every time. She asked me if I was interested in cattle, and I said yes, which was practically my undoing. The man in the black hat and with the black moustache jumped up and came over. He was emaciated and moved swiftly, still chewing the food, a long spaghetti hanging from his mouth, his lips working hard, trying to suck in the spaghetti. Before I had time to appreciate what it entailed, he decided that he would take me twelve miles on foot the next day to see a large herd of Salers which was leaving for the mountains.

In spring the cattle leaves for the mountains and comes back in autumn. I have read of cattle which, when the weather was too bad for their liking, came back to the stables without asking leave. The man in the black hat assured me there would be at least sixty cows, as pleasing a sight as I could wish for. But the next morning I wasn't in the mood for setting out with him. I left the red cows, walked to the Grande Place, and there he was waiting for me, his chin covered in butter, his black hat grey with dust in the sunshine. I told him I didn't feel up to it; besides, I had seen near the workhouse all the cows I wanted to see. He said he would bring two walking-sticks: one for himself, one for me. I said I didn't want to see the cows; he retaliated it was too late now because the sticks were waiting. I said let them wait; he said they wouldn't. He was so disillusioned that saliva squirted from his mouth. He let it rest on his chin, and said in that case he would leave the sticks behind, but would take me to a farm near the workhouse where there was some cattle too. I said I had just come from that farm. He lost his temper and we parted.

When I had left him and walked towards the gate of La Martille, which has a tower above it, a tower shorter but resembling that of the belfry, I met Mimi. She came up to me as one comes up to an intimate friend to tell him something that is for his ears alone and shouldn't be repeated. She had greying fair hair, the nose was aquiline, the eyes those of a lamb. She wore slippers, a dusty black dress, which was too small for her, and stockings riddled with holes.

"Do you want to make a million a month?" she asked. Naturally I blushed. It was too sudden; and who doesn't want a million a month? "You can make it," she continued in a confidential voice, "by sending food to Russia and to England. But you must send it underground, because there are the Arabs who strangle young men." She lost interest in money and food. "Young men," she sighed. "They are all in love with me. So many of them commit suicide. For me, of course. I was married three times, but sent all my husbands packing."

At that moment Mimi saw a man and a dog coming towards us. She darted away, ran up to the man and asked him whether he wanted to make a million francs a month. In the course of my chats with the inhabitants I pieced together Mimi's story. She was sixty-eight years old. She had been pretty and normal, so they said. But, alas, she read too many novels and at the age of eighteen she went mad, and a few years later was despatched to a lunatic asylum. "But," said the secretary of the mayor of Salers, "she got out in an elegant fashion. She made so much noise, behaved so badly that they were only too glad to let her go." She came home to Salers; her parents were dead, and she has stayed in Salers ever since, living on public and private charity, living in the tower of La Martille, sacks her bedding; and she is unmolested, humoured, in fact the town considers her as one of its historic monuments. "If anything happened to her," said the secretary, "Salers wouldn't be the same." Women of the town gave her their old dresses, and she would be given breakfast here, midday soup there. The people at my hotel gave her supper every evening, which made me change my opinion of them up to a point. Of course, she was never married; nevertheless, she still considered herself desirable. She wasn't without cunning, and if anybody was rude to her, or she felt herself slighted, she would rake up dark secrets of that person's past and in a loud voice for all Salers to hear, tax him with them nimbly. I saw her again, darting about, running to and fro, happy and pleased with life and Mimi.

After I left Mimi I went to Mass. The church of Salers

deeply moved me. It had been begun in the thirteenth century, was added to through the ages, was rebuilt now and then, the doorway, however, remaining pure Romanesque, the tower rebuilt in the last century, after the original tower had been destroyed by lightning. In the church are five excellent Aubusson tapestries, given to the church in 1534. That date is considered wrong by experts of tapestry, but local historians grimly stick to it. What impressed me most and will remain unforgettable in my memory because of its sheer beauty, is the Mise au Tombeau, sculptured by unknown artists of the Burgundian School; the date is put at 1495.

The painted stone figures are almost frighteningly alive; when I say frighteningly I mean one feels the misery of those who were putting Our Lord into his tomb. The Mother of God, so young and beautiful, yet so sad; and one waits for her tears. Martha, Elisabeth and Mary Magdalen would like to console her, but their own grief is too strong. The boyish St. John holds out his arm as if to steady Our Lady. They are all richly clad and desperate. Joseph of Arimathea and Nicodemus hold the shroud, and one waits for them to let Our Lord gently into the tomb. As a matter of fact, after a few minutes one can't understand why they don't move. On the side stands a bored man: the guardian of the tomb. I went back at least ten times to the Mise au Tombeau, and each time I half expected to find Our Lord already in the tomb, and hoped that resignation would take the place of deep despair in the mourners. The dead Christ is anatomically perfect. As I stood and gazed at Him I was reminded of the words of Monsieur Laverdet of Souillac. "God," he had said to me on one occasion, "has hidden in His mercy the meaning of death from us." The dead Christ in the shroud knew the meaning.

Vic-sur-Cère

Salers: the Old Square

Mise au Tombeau, Church of Salers

Twelfth-Century Tympanum, Church of Souillac

It is rather disappointing to listen to the experts and not to the enthusiastic local historians who, as I have said, give the date of the tapestries as 1534. One tapestry represents St. Ignatius of Loyola at the altar with two saints, probably St. Francis Xavier and St. Luis Gonzaga. On the panel is the monogram of the Jesuits, I.H.S., with the cross with three nails. Yet the experts maintain that those tapestries are after 1610 because one figure wears the garb of the Visitandines, a religious order started by St. François de Sales in 1610; and one can't argue with those who know. Outside the church on the north side is a Pietà of the fifteenth century. When before the war some old houses were demolished in the Place de l'Église, an antique dealer suggested to the mayor he should sell him the Pietà for a fabulous sum, and he, the dealer, would have an exact replica made. The townsfolk wouldn't notice the difference. The mayor laughed and that was the end of it.

The mother of the curé having died two days before, Mass was celebrated by the young abbé with whom I had travelled from Aurillac. The church was full, and if, as it is believed, a Frenchman is a radical and an atheist as long as his wife goes regularly to confession, and there is time left for deathbed repentance, then all I can say is that it doesn't hold good in Salers, nor in the rest of Auvergne, which is a deeply religious land, where faith is alive and part and parcel of daily life.

Most of that Sunday afternoon I spent in a café facing the church. The proprietress, a tall woman with dark hair and blue eyes, talked to me of Salers, the way of life in Salers and of the inhabitants. I sat and listened to her, a simple woman who hadn't been often out of the town. She had a daughter in Paris, a daughter she worshipped, yet she hadn't seen her for a year, because Paris was far, noisy and it alarmed her. During the hot afternoon that woman talked to me for hours. In the café a few men in their Sunday black were playing écarté, as if belotte hadn't yet reached Salers. She spoke with admirable precision, she instinctively used the right word, and her French was grammatically and syntactically perfect. It was a pleasure to listen to her. Of last winter, which had been cold and laden with snow, she said: "For four months we didn't see the earth." A farmer came up to interrupt her and spoke to her in patois, she answered in French, so the farmer spoke in French too.

Next morning I was taken round the town by the secretary of the mayor. He was a large man with a protruding belly, little hair, a round head, a ginger moustache, and he wore a dark suit and slippers. He was from the industrial North, and I, who was so completely inside my palisade, thought he came from north of Clermont. Only on second thoughts I perceived that he meant the North of France. "When I came here," he said, "all I wanted was to stay as little as possible. Now I know I will die here. You see, those stones turning from black to grey in summer, and back to black in winter, have got hold of me, and will keep me here for good." I almost saw his point. He was a man of erudition, and not only answered knowledgeably my somewhat complicated questions, but anticipated them. He rolled a cigarette even while we were in the church.

The wind of history hadn't shaken Salers unduly. It was originally called Salern, and an effort was made to try and find a connection between Salers and Salerno, especially as St. Matthew is the patron saint of both towns. He, the secretary, attached no importance to that. The first baron of Salers lived around 1069, the third baron went to the Crusade in 1095; and those are the first two dates in the history of the town. The Hundred Years' Wars, and most of the feudal rivalries and fights Salers escaped, and lived on in comparative quiet with the barons of Salers, whose fortified castle was outside the town. The English came in 1357. The inhabitants fled to the castle, which the English couldn't take. They took, however, their cattle, and even then Salers had so much cattle that the English didn't know what to do with it, and they weren't large enough in number to drive it all away, and thus the cattle became a cumbersome problem. But the English solved it in a practical manner, that is they sold back to the inhabitants every beast they didn't need.

"You see," said the secretary, rolling a cigarette, "the English had already a commercial sense."

The English came back several times, probably to do more business.

The Routiers came in 1427 and sacked the town. The following year the town was fortified. The fortifications ended with the towers of the belfry and of La Martille, the church remaining outside the walls, and round the church grew the new town, the inhabitants of which in case of trouble could find refuge either in the fortified town or in the castle. In the fortified town were the houses of several noblemen—the houses I had admired. At some time or other the Templars had been in Salers, but all that is known of them is that they sold a house, a building which now houses the Catholic school, and it has an imposing Gothic passage, Gothic turning into Rennaissance again. The nobles of Salers stayed in the town only during summer. They were landowners from the Limousin, or the Creuse, or the Corrèze. They were well-to-do but not rich, and their houses were without luxury. As time went by the houses changed hands, and judges and notaries came in the place of the landowners.

Of the Protestant attack I have already spoken. When Cardinal Richelieu decided in the course of his journey through Auvergne to have the castles of the great nobles destroyed and thus put an end to all feudal ideas, Salers wasn't left out, and the castle was pulled down in 1666. The Revolution didn't leave Salers unscathed, though the Terror didn't trammel it too much. In the Maison de la Ronade lived an old lady with her two sons, both officers in the King's Army. They escaped at the beginning of the Terror. The old lady was told she was responsible for the disappearance of her sons, and was accordingly guillotined at the age of seventy-two. I shook my head.

"Ah," said the secretary, "that Revolution was a curious business, and no historian has really explained it. Not to my satisfaction, at any rate. A revolution of lawyers assisted by the mob. . . ." It was his turn to shake his head.

We went and drank white wine in a café, then he took me into a fifteenth-century house. We climbed the stairs. The house was a bit like a slum. The next house had a balcony with three arches. "Saracen influence," he said. "I can't explain it, but I feel it is Saracen."

"Makes me feel near to the Mediterranean," I said, then remarked the nobles who had lived in Salers hadn't extravagant tastes to judge by the size of their houses.

"The houses suited their needs," was his very French reply.

He had to leave me to go to his office. We drank a last glass of white wine and I thanked him gratefully. He said he had enjoyed it as much as I did. The population of Salers was of true kindness to me. Everybody was helpful, and the story that the Auvergnat is dour didn't hold good in Salers. Before luncheon a peasant offered me a drink in a café but then went off to talk to a friend, so I paid for my drink, left for the hotel, and on my return I found he was waiting for me. "Why did you pay for that drink?" he asked. "Who do you think I am? A brigand?"

We had a drink, and in order to make conversation I inquired from him whether the fair weather would stay or rain would come back.

"I am no geologist," he said, "so I can't answer your question."

I made a final pilgrimage to the Gendarmerie Nationale, though it had nothing to do with the gendarmes. The window of the Gendarmerie is a superb Renaissance window, and the more often I looked at it the more difficult it was to tear myself away. Beside the window was a recruiting poster for the French Colonial Infantry.

While I was waiting for the bus two fat men had an argument in the square. One of the fat men told the other either he paid him by next market day the hundred thousand francs he owed him, or he would take action against him. The other fat man said it was impolite to shout like that in public, and they both rushed out of earshot. In a little while they came back and had a drink. It seemed unlikely that either the money would be paid back by next market day or any action would be taken. They were still drinking when the bus left. It was hot in the bus, but the windows were open, and soon we were out of Salers; and I already felt homesick for the black town.

Chapter Six

VIC-SUR-CÈRE

THE bus was loaded with women. Apparently women alone went to Salers and came from Salers. We reached Mauriac after an hour's journey. It was according to my itinerary my next stop. The driver accompanied me to the best hotel, the hotel recommended by the secretary of the Syndicat in Aurillac. The driver thought I would certainly like it, and I was longing for a comfortable hotel, especially longing for cleanliness and decent sanitation. We climbed a rotting wooden staircase, we were inside a house that was rotting too. It was dark, the long passage was lit by one bulb. Outside it was three o'clock in the afternoon. Inside the house the hour seemed ripe for ghosts to fall on me, and dance with me against my wish. We reached the kitchen, in which a solitary man was eating. He wore a white jacket, and spoke civilly. He was the hotel proprietor. I inquired about sanitation. He said there was none to speak of. Though I knew I was upsetting my time-table, I thanked him and said I was sorry but I wouldn't stay. He thanked me and said he was sorry too. He sat down and went on with his meal. The driver carried my luggage back to the bus stop. There was a bus for Aurillac later on in the afternoon. At Aurillac I could take the auto-rail to Vic-sur-Cère. I wasn't pleased with the thought of having to go to Aurillac again; in fact, I felt as if Aurillac had become an unwanted new background of my life.

Since I had two hours to kill, I took a quick look at the town. Perhaps if I hadn't been to Salers, Mauriac might have impressed me. It didn't. It was the sort of town that

158

lives only on market day: on other days the quiet streets are
asleep, and don't seem even to be waiting for the hour of
awakening, that is for market day.

The houses are of basalt, but no patch on Salers. My
mind was full of Salers: Salers was my yardstick. The
Basilique of Nôtre-Dame-des-Miracles is considered to be
the purest example of Romanesque architecture in Auvergne; and here I must make a shameful confession. I
didn't go into the Basilique. It isn't inexplicable. I had
visited many churches and houses, many of which had, as
the saying goes, bowled me over, especially those of Salers.
There comes, in my case at any rate, a moment when one
can take in no more fine buildings, in short one is saturated.
I had frequently felt like that in picture galleries. Twenty
paintings can inspire me, after that I am just counting the
number of canvases. The hour that was still at my disposal I spent lazily in a café near the bus stop.

I was joined by my friend the peasant, the one who had
told me he was no geologist. It is not without charm to sit
and watch the life of a town one is probably never going to
see again. One is detached, aloof yet ready to be amused.
There were many peasants about, they were going in and out
of cafés and drank a lot, stood in small groups, buses came,
buses went, a young woman got into a bus, going in all
likelihood no farther than the next town; none the less her
entire family accompanied her, goodbye kisses and embraces
were fervent, and the young woman waved till the bus
turned the corner. It appeared to me, as I sat there idly,
that the parochial life of France, and especially as I found it
in the Cantal, is one of the strongest bulwarks both of
France and of the French nation. Apart from military
service they seldom leave their district. Those men and
women who came and went before my eyes were bent on
small errands and journeys, and they were within the

frontiers of their small lives. The smaller those lives perhaps the more contentment they hold. I wouldn't know, but watching them bent on their limited and short purposes they seemed less miserable than so many others whose horizons and circuits are wider.

My bus came, a brand new cream-coloured affair, and a crowd gathered to admire it. Twenty minutes to wait; nevertheless, the crowd remained patiently near the bus. In the café they talked only of the bus, and it was the sort of technical conversation which motor-car bores favour. My thoughts were far from the bus.

In the eighth century, at the time of the Saracen invasion, the inhabitants of Mauriac woke up one morning to find two men in chains before the basilica. The men were eagerly questioned and their answer was that they had been made prisoners by the infidels, and in their prison cell they prayed to the Mother of God to liberate them, and the night before they had prayed with great fervour again, then fell asleep, and they woke up in Mauriac. Those chains, now called the Saracen Chains, are carried in procession on the Feast of the Virgin, which in Mauriac is on the eighth of May.

Pace Mauriac, I said to myself, but why did those two prisoners want to exchange their cell for Mauriac of all places? I laughed alone at my table, and the peasants looked at me and concluded I was mad.

It was time to get into the bus. I sat near the driver, who changed gear clumsily, and apologised for doing so. He explained with becoming modesty that he was still unaccustomed to driving so modern a bus. There was the usual load of women in black, a few peasants, commercial travellers, and in front of me sat a woman dressed according to urban fashion. She was covered in scent; a little boy was car-sick. The driver wasn't pleased yet comforted the parents.

"Disgusting," said the woman, turning to me, and went on to ask me a host of questions. Was I a foreigner? Did I know Paris? What was I doing in the Cantal? Wasn't the Cantal awful in comparison to Paris? She boasted of her gay and expensive life in Paris. The Tour d'Argent followed Maxim's, and then she spoke of another restaurant, which, she lamented, was too cheap. One could eat there for six thousand francs per head. She shook her head. The pastures were alive with the cows of Tout Salers, but she didn't give them even a glance. The bus rolled proudly through small villages, the mountains kept in step with us, viaducts, rivers and waterfalls followed regularly, and she looked at her diamond-studded watch. The bus reached a farm; in front of the farm stood an old peasant and an old peasant woman. The farm building was dilapidated. The bus stopped, the lady from Maxim's jumped out, ran up to the two old people and the three of them embraced. Before the bus left they were already on their way to the peasant's abode; she had already taken her hat off.

We reached Aurillac around six o'clock. It was raining. I waited for the auto-rail at the station, for I was disinclined to go back to the town. When the auto-rail pulled out what I had mostly in my mind was that I shouldn't have to come back to Aurillac. I was grateful. The auto-rail's route was beside the Cère, and mountains were on each side of river and rails. There were mountains in front too. It looked as if we were approaching a tunnel, but at the last moment the mountains in front gave way. They repeated that several times. Vic-sur-Cère is the second station after Aurillac. I decided to forget the list of hotels supplied by the secretary of the Syndicat d'Initiatives at Aurillac, and to strike out on my own. Nevertheless, I inquired at the station what the hotel the secretary had recommended was like, that is I asked if it had a bathroom.

I wanted a bathroom: that was all I wanted. Certainly, but it wouldn't be in use before the season began. Vic is a watering-place. I went to the best hotel.

Vic is an extraordinary town. It would have delighted Henry James, and Proust would probably have liked it. It is a sad town because its days of glory are gone; and the glory couldn't have amounted to much. Nowadays only those visit Vic who can't afford Vichy. The past lingers on: it is made up of disappeared landaus, parasols, obscene bellies, beards and sloping shoulders. Manet could be in the picture, but not Toulouse-Lautrec. At the present time Vic is vulgar and, in deference to the past, genteel too. It is like a crooked finger beside a chipped teacup. The genteel side of the town has no truck with Auvergne; the vulgar is alive and embedded in the Cantal. The genteel town regrets its past. The municipal council, however, has a majority of rich peasants and, outvoting the tradesmen, they refuse to revive the past. The first thing I noticed as I reached the high street was that the town was as divided as the municipal council. On one side of the street were the hotels and the shops catering for the visitor, on the other side were shops and bistros for the use of the townsfolk and the peasants of the district. Thus the hotel side was tattered Edwardian, whereas the other was timeless, like the peasant. That division I found quite amusing.

The best hotel in town is the Hôtel Vialette. Madame Vialette took me to my room. I nearly burst into tears of gratitude: so clean it all was. I almost kissed the carpeted staircase. Few things give as much pleasure as comfort if one missed it for a few days: yet one goes calmly to war, stays without comfort for years, and when returning one is more surprised than pleased. Precisely; and that is why I was impressed by the armchair in my room, and the white towels enraptured me. I found the hotel agreeable; it belonged to the past, of which the carpet on the stairs was the chief representative. The food wasn't remarkable, but the hotel guests, with my exception, had come to Vic for the cure. They were a quiet lot: bank clerks and typists of mature age. It didn't occur to me till well afterwards that they weren't looking only after their livers but were partaking of their enjoyable yearly holiday, which, frankly, they took as sadly as decorum permitted.

The season was still in the offing, so we ate in the small dining-room. At one table sat an old man who wore dark glasses indoors. With him was an old woman who limped. They sat side by side, that is they faced me. They took, probably unknown to them, a violent dislike to me. When I came into the dining-room they hated me; their eyes didn't leave me while I ate; and when I left their hatred followed me to the door. One day I saw them in the street, and I became aware of them only when I was already within the circle of their hatred. At another table was a yellow-faced woman, middle-aged and given to gushing. She gushed over the same two daffodils that adorned her table every day; gushed over the food, each course receiving loud, exaggerated praise. Madame Vialette was the centre of her gushing. Whenever she came into the dining-room the yellow face well-nigh scintillated. At a table near the door sat a man who blew his nose. He blew it as he made his entrance, blew it before and after each dish; then he blew it with his coffee. A fat woman with one arm was the last guest.

The hotel guests would, after luncheon, go out and sit on the verandah, and if they took to the streets, I feel certain, walked strictly on the hotel side of the high street. Several local tradesmen talked to me of the past glory of Vic. On account of the hotel guests it was difficult for me to visualise those lost great days.

Undaunted by my experience in Aurillac, I sought out the Syndicat. The building that housed the Syndicat was on the way to the station. I went there first thing on the first morning. It was a wooden hut off the road, and inside I found a little old man with an enormous moustache, the sort of moustache which takes over the wearer's individuality. It is moustache this, and moustache that, and the man fades out of the picture. It was in fact the moustache that told me that Vic was a spa. What else? I asked. Excursions. Not for me. Railway time-table. I said I didn't need it. The little man, happily ensconced behind the moustache, stared at me uncomprehendingly, then a thought came to him. I should go and see a certain person at the Mairie who knew a good deal about the history of the town. I thanked him, left him, found the Mairie but not my man. He had left Vic two years ago. That was annoying; however, it threw a new light on the moustache. To live in a tiny place like Vic and to be unaware of the departure of a fellow town-dweller showed the aloofness of the moustache.

My sole informant in Vic was the proprietress of a café. She was a cosy, fat woman, endowed with understanding and wit. She apologised for her lack of education, also for having forgotten most of the little she had learned at school. Yet she was full of information and talked intelligently. It was no fault of hers that I had a door banged in my face that evening.

She told me there lived a learned man in Vic, a man thoroughly acquainted with the history of the town. She suggested I should go and see him, she would accompany me—the best time was after dinner, around nine o'clock. I dined at the hotel face to face with the hatred of the old man and his old wife. After dinner I strolled to the bistro. It was a warm evening and the town was packing up for the night. The cafés were empty, though the lights still burned in them. The mountains had already gone to sleep. My friend was waiting for me in her bistro. An elderly man dozed near the billiard table, and to him she entrusted the bistro, without bothering to tell him so. We left. The learned man lived in a twisting, narrow old street. She rang the bell, there was no sound, she rang again.

"Probably," I said, "he isn't in."

"Everybody is in at this time of the evening."

We heard footsteps, they ceased and the door opened slowly. In the doorway stood a man, but all the darkness vouchsafed me was a slim figure. His face I didn't see. The kind woman explained my errand. I intended to write a book on Auvergne, should be grateful for any information, and the man took a step back, lifted both arms; the hands were like hands painted by Greco, hands wishing to push evil away. The light of a distant bulb was on the hands which were grappling with the devil.

"Never," he screeched, "never. I got all my knowledge in the archives at Aurillac. I worked for it; it belongs to me. It is mine." He was now hissing. "Yes, mine. Never. It is mine and I won't give it. Oh no." He cackled ironically. "Oh no, nothing doing. Mine. Yes, mine. Please go. Good night."

The door banged in our faces. I for one was blushing, feeling like a fool and a thief who had been caught at it. My friend simply shrugged her shoulders.

"He is in a bad mood," she said. "At other times he can be very pleasant."

By then I was smiling; for an irresistible picture had enfolded before me. In a vast world bent on vast pursuits sat a man on his knowledge, knowledge nobody beside me needed in the vast world. He sat on it and wouldn't part with it, albeit it was of little importance even for me. There were enough reference books at my disposal. Perhaps because one could do so easily without it gave him that strong sense of property.

"Life is so quiet and uneventful here," said my friend, "that one exaggerates all the time."

There, I suppose, she was right. The *vita contemplativa* doesn't make one a good mixer. Edward Fitzgerald indulged in it, and one of its results was a fair amount of boorishness.

I returned with her to the bistro, where, in order to make up for our unsuccessful call, she gave me the little she knew of local history. We were alone in the bistro, no car disturbed the silence of the street. First she laughed, then she said the Reine Margot had had many lovers. Not only lovers but a bathtub too. She was one up on Salers, I said to myself. At any rate the bathtub was filled on occasions with eau de Cologne, that is whenever a shepherd or a herdsman was brought into her bed. Before he was commanded to make love to her he had to dip himself in the tub.

"I wish," she said, "they would still dip themselves, especially on market days." She thought for a moment. "But, of course, they would only do it for a queen." She laughed.

It was at Vic that the Reine Margot saw the Auvergnat dance called *la bourrée*, which she so much enjoyed that through her it reached the Court of France, and was danced at Versailles even in the days of Louis XIV.

She spoke of Coffinhal, a local lawyer, who during the Revolution headed the Terror in the Cantal. "He had," she said, "a strong taste for the guillotine." Coffinhal made a good thing out of the Terror. His daughter bought an aristocrat with her dowry. She told me too of an old miser who had lived at Vic. One day he lost the power of speech; by then he was old and bedridden. He would lie in bed and point at the wall, point at it in despair. He died still pointing, as it were, at the wall. The heirs rushed to the wall, almost pulled the house down, but nothing was found. The house nowadays is called the house of the treasure.

My friend tried hard to remember other anecdotes, and she came out with one more. The Routiers had sacked the town, left their hoard in a cave near the town. They went away to loot and rape elsewhere and never came back to fetch the hoard. "Perhaps," she added, "that isn't true. I don't remember it well."

The next day at luncheon I had an edifying conversation with the hotel proprietress. She had heard from my friend in the bistro that I was writing a book on Auvergne. That she considered an excellent idea. What Auvergne needed was publicity, and the watering-place of Vic needed it especially. She was, she declared, a businessman; in fact, she knew what she was speaking of. Business was business, and one had to spend money if one wanted to make money. Did I approve? I said I certainly approved, though I didn't know what she was driving at. I soon found out. If I wrote up the town and chiefly her hotel she would pay me. She had a friend, a lawyer, and we could all get together and then get down to it and discuss the figure. She wouldn't make an offer before she consulted him. Beads of perspiration galloped down her pale cheeks. She was visibly afraid I would ask for too much; and frightened that by offering too little she should lose her chance; and, besides, could I be trusted, would I truly write the book? And if I wrote it would anybody read it? And if it was read would it induce anybody to go to Vic? And what if the reader went to some other hotel? She was leaning forward, her eyes on me, and her fingers were twitching. She lifted the ash-tray, then put it down.

I assured her she had no reason to give me any money.

The book would be only a reflection of my likes and dislikes. I liked her hotel, therefore I certainly would mention it, and that was all I would or could do for her. She was, I suggested, thinking of guide books. Mine wouldn't be a guide book. It took me some time to explain that I wasn't a camouflaged collector of advertisements. She seemed disappointed, for she had expected to pay; I stopped her, and she felt that somehow or other it was she who was the loser. Earmarked money is unquiet in the purse. She remained pleasant to me for the rest of my stay, but wasn't interested in me any more.

She wasn't alone in suspecting me of writing that sort of book. In the beginning of my unfinished journey I observed, and was surprised by, a certain coldness which overtook hotel and restaurant keepers when I mentioned to them that I intended to write about Auvergne. Now I understood. Those people are often pestered by fellows who wish to bring out guide books, guides to towns, to restaurants and hotels, and they come and eat copiously, drink more than might be good for them, collect money for advertisements, and often enough the book doesn't even appear.

The light sadness of the town accounts partly for its charm: the old houses and the mountains make one's stay memorable. The finicky, genteel hotels seem to shudder when cattle is driven through the streets. At the end of the high street I found a small bar. The barkeeper was a dark Auvergnat. He asked me how I liked the hotel, I said very much; he said he let rooms and his food was better. He was willing to make special terms if I moved into his house. That sort of offer abounded during my journey through the Cantal, and I had the impression that one became a desirable guest only after one had established oneself elsewhere.

The old houses of the town are in the Cardalez style, symmetric windows, and pointed roofs, covered with heavy

grey tiles. The streets are tortuous, and many of them are
without light. If one leaves the town in the direction of Le
Lioran, one is expected to reach a waterfall. I went, lost my
way, didn't find the waterfall but wandered about in the
countryside. It was a hot day, the mountain range oozed
with heat. I reached a small village, dusty and smelling of
cow dung. I found a bistro, which wasn't much of a bistro;
it was the living-room of the family with a few bottles
ranged on a table. I asked for a glass of red wine, and while
I drank it four men came in. They were slightly drunk,
and very noisy. They sat down at the table at which I sat.
They didn't see me. A bottle of wine was put before them;
they drank, chatted loudly in patois and I was ignored.
It wasn't rudeness, nor bad manners. I wasn't of the neighbourhood and that was all.

I walked on in the heat which sat heavily on the valley of
the Cère. I thought of returning to Vic beside the river,
thus I wouldn't miss the waterfall. The water looked cool,
a few sheep grazed in a meadow, a woman drove a goat on
the other side of the river, a few head of red cattle were on
the hillside, the sun caressed a distant cemetery and then
the road came to an end. There were rocks alone before me,
moreover the river had disappeared behind the rocks. I
climbed the hillside and went into the cemetery. One can
learn a lot in a cemetery. In that cemetery it was evident
again that Auvergne had bred through the turbulent centuries a vast crop of small nobility. In the cemetery, which
dated back to the beginning of the eighteenth century, there
was hardly a name without a ''de'' before it. It is, I believe,
owing to the small nobility that lay architecture survived in
Auvergne. They, the small nobles, went into the towns and
left the feudal lords to their cruelty, ambition, rapacious-
ness in their fortified castles till Cardinal de Richelieu
ordered their castles to be demolished. Consequently of the

castles ruins alone remain, whereas in the towns the unpretentious, elegant houses of the small nobility survive.

An old man came into the cemetery. He was a dignified old man in gaiters, tall and erect. He went up to a grave, crossed himself and stood motionless. I wanted to ask him the direction to the waterfall, but hadn't the courage to disturb him. He left after a while, and curiosity led me to the grave. It was the tomb of a young man of twenty, killed at Verdun thirty-five years ago. I walked back to Vic along the main road, thus never saw the waterfall.

The next day I went for another walk which was more tiring. Above Vic is a rock on the top of the mountain called the Rocher des Pendus. Apparently brigands and highwaymen had been hanged there in the good old days. I was urged to climb to the rock because the view is magnificent. I am no climber, therefore had no intention to climb the steep mountain; moreover, it was hot. But I went for a stroll that afternoon, walked past the station, walked up a few hundred yards beside a stream. I passed a farm, met a tiny waterfall, wandered on and saw a signpost. The signpost had been put up by the Touring Club de France. It said: forty-five minutes to the rock. Somehow that became an unexpected challenge. It was a childish challenge, a challenge I should have ignored since I am no mountaineer, had no desire to climb the rock, and it was hot and I was completely given to laziness. The challenge persisted, and thirty-five minutes later, a panting, lazy person with his lungs almost bursting, his heart past thumping, arrived triumphantly on the top of the rock. My ten minutes' victory over the allotted time was for the moment my most cherished trophy.

The view was indeed superb. The town beneath me a conglomeration of pointed roofs, the Puy-Mary in the distance an interplay of snow and majesty, the snow virgin-like

in the sun. Yet it wasn't the view alone that brings me
back the Rock of the Hanged. Standing up there, looking
round up there, I had for inexplicable reasons a brief picture
of Auvergne burning, as it had burned in the Tertiary Age
when the Pyrénées and the Alps rose from the bowels of the
earth. There is something grandiose though frightening in
trying to visualise a world with which one has naught in
common. It is terrifying to conjure up a world which is
based sheerly on the power of the elements. At sea one has
now and then such a feeling but is reassured by the fact that
the ship is seaworthy, and also by the statistics which prove
that only a few ships go down in a storm. But Auvergne
burning, with no fire engines, no firemen's ladder, no
asbestos and no statistics of the insurance companies to
fall back on, was a picture that filled me with awe; and
as I stood there, still panting, on the top of the Rock of the
Hanged, I felt, as perhaps I had never felt before, the peace
God gave man to be disrupted but by man. And He had
tamed the elements for us to be able to live unmolested on
earth. To undo His peace He left it entirely to us. Perhaps more than Auvergne will burn if we continue on our
path. The blue sky, the snow on Puy-Mary and the Cère
in the valley seemed detached from my thoughts.

I had to admit, however, that the mass of burning volcanoes, burning wildly because they weren't to last, was a
fine picture. At night; and, according to the story already
mentioned, the Auvergnat stood in his black suit, black
hat, waiting with a rapacious smile for the volcanoes to go
out, waiting patiently, eating Cantal, when bored dancing
the *Bourrée*, and preparing himself to take over when the
going would be good.

I left the rock and went to a small inn, where, after my
mountaineering feat, I thought I deserved a drink. I was
hungry too. The inn was dismal, though it was a warm

day with the sun doing his duty, the parlour was heavy with washing. Shirts, mended and patched, hung on lines. The smell of *eau de Javel* was strong. From underneath a patched petticoat the innkeeper appeared. I asked for beer. He said he expected delivery of beer any day. The season, he explained, hadn't yet begun, so he was in no hurry. That business of seasons makes travelling in France often obnoxious. It has become as much a factor and as delineated as, say, sowing or reaping. As the countryman wouldn't sow in February, so the innkeeper wouldn't lay in beer before the season began. One should, consequently, travel but during the season, and then one would be surrounded by caravans, charabancs, crowds, bad service and possibly nowhere to put one's head.

I waved beer aside and drank a glass of wine. I asked whether he had anything to eat, such as sausage or cheese. No, but by the first of July he would have everything. A tiny battered car stopped before the inn. A short man came in, asking the innkeeper whether he wanted to buy a certain brand of aperitif, the innkeeper said he didn't, and because it was a feat of glory to climb to the rock but boring anticlimax to walk down, I inquired if the short man was on his way to Vic. He politely offered to drive me to Vic as it was on his way. I rid myself of petticoats and shirts, and followed him to his car. We drove off, and the short man, who had huge sad black eyes, told me at once that he was an Albanian. He told me that as if he were doing me the favour of driving me to Vic under false pretences if he hadn't acquainted me with his origin. "But," he added quickly, "I'm a naturalised Frenchman, my wife is French, and of course my son is French. My wife is from Paris, you know."

"Yes, indeed," I said. It is difficult to answer, so to speak, statements in which one isn't interested.

"You see," he went on, "I came to France at the age of nineteen, so frankly I consider myself a Frenchman. There is nothing I want more than to be taken for a Frenchman. I understood French life straightaway. It is very intellectual and full of *esprit*. My friends—they're all French—say I have the real *esprit Gaulois*. Make a witty remark and I shall cap it without having to think even for a second. That is very French. My wife often tells me that she has completely forgotten that she married a foreigner." He laughed. "Mind you, when she is angry she tells me to go back to the Balkans." He pulled himself together. "I was only joking. Of course she never says that. What would my son think of me if he were told I came from the Balkans?" We were driving along a winding road, which here and there cut through the path that had led me to the rock. "The reason," he continued, "I love France is because it is my real country. Do you know what my wife and I do on Sundays?" I let that pass, since there is so much a husband and a wife could do on a Sunday. "I'll tell you. You see I travel the whole week and get back to Paris on Sunday. Cantal is my furthest district. I do the Puy-de-Dome, the Haute Loire, the Allier and the Nièvre. A lot you will admit, but my firm trusts me. I do good business for the firm. Here we are. Do come into this bistro with me. You will have a drink with me."

The air was cooler, the trees near the river were letting out their shadows, and I had a completely empty evening before me. I accompanied him to the bistro. He knew the proprietor, the proprietor said he needed nothing before the first of July, but in July he would certainly want six bottles. The Albanian asked me to have a drink and, needless to say, offered me a glass of his firm's brand of apéritif. It was too sweet for my liking, but out of gratitude for my lift, and because I had taken to him, I praised the drink.

"I don't drink it," he said. "I am a philosopher. I think it is far better to be detached from what one sells. Like that I can praise it unreservedly." I was reminded of a publisher whose success, so the wags had it, was based on his never having read a book he published. "Now then, what were we talking about in the car? It was such an interesting conversation."

A monologue is invariably interesting for him who speaks.

"You were going to tell me," I said, "what you and your wife do on Sundays."

"That's it. Well, I come back to Paris on Saturday night, tired, believe me, very tired. One doesn't meet such good talkers like you every day. Frankly, one has to talk to some very uneducated people. So I arrive home on Saturday night, very tired. I have a good night's rest, but it isn't enough. Then comes Sunday. We eat a very copious dinner, my wife, my son and I. Then I say to my wife: 'What would you like to do?' I suggest going, say, to the Gaumont Palace, or sitting outside a café if the day is fine, in fact anything she would like. But my wife usually says: 'Let's stay at home.' And do you know what we do? We go to bed and stay there the whole afternoon. I sleep a little, do my accounts, she reads a book, then we chat, and," he had nearly tears in his eyes, "you can't believe how peaceful it is. I wouldn't give up those Sunday afternoons for a million. No, I wouldn't."

And I saw before me shooting and knifing in his native land on Sunday afternoons. Perhaps a couple of houses blazing too.

"I'm sure you wouldn't," I said.

He asked me what I did in life. I said I wrote books, and he was impressed.

"You can," he said, "talk to me on serious subjects.

History, geography, French literature and so on. My son goes to the *lycée*. I read all his school books, so you can talk to me. My son is thirteen years old."

Another commercial traveller came in, and sat down with us. Conversation became tepid. The new arrival mentioned among other personal items that he had been to Salers the day before. I was still full of Salers, so I said the Mise au Tombeau of Salers was one of the most moving things I had seen in my life.

"Where is that?" asked the newcomer.

"In the church," I said.

"Is it interesting?"

"It couldn't be compared with a Wild West picture," I said, and repented at once. It is quite unforgivable to poke fun at people because they haven't the acquired taste of appreciating beauty.

"I prefer the cinema," he laughed, and I saw the only person to whom I owed an apology was my better self.

That evening I looked at the time-table the secretary of the Syndicat in Aurillac had made out for me, and I saw without sorrow that the next day I could in all conscience leave Vic. It seemed to me, as I lay in bed waiting for sleep to hoist me to the morning, that Vic was a curious place. Fundamentally it had little to do with Auvergne. Notwithstanding the visits of the Routiers, in spite of the Wars of Religion, it was an urbane spot which should be on a more accessible road. It had been put into my jungle for no apparent reason. It should be, say, on the road from Paris to Vichy. But in that case the mountains couldn't accompany it, the Cère would remain behind, and the Puy-Mary wouldn't even think of going along with it. Geographically, I concluded, too many facts would have to be eliminated for the word if to come into play; and then, as in history, nothing might be left.

In the morning I asked for my bill. The hotel proprietress made out the bill. It was reasonable. She said she gave me a reduction because I was a writer.

"And don't forget," she said, looking young and coy, "to write nicely about my hotel."

I promised I would do so. There remained but to say goodbye to the kind woman who had spoken of Coffinhal's taste for the guillotine. We parted perfunctorily, which was no fault of mine. Is it possible that her Auvergnat soul already repented of having given secrets of Auvergne away?

Chapter Seven

MURAT AND SAINT-FLOUR

I HAD decided, because it was on my itinerary, to visit Le Lioran on my way to Murat. The visit would take one day, that is arriving in the morning and going on to Murat in the evening. Le Lioran, I knew, had no old churches and old buildings to offer. It was a tourist centre for winter sports. It is at the altitude of one thousand one hundred and one metres, on the other side of a long tunnel, with a few hotels and restaurants. There would still be snow, and pines abounded. I should, so I was warned, be deeply moved by the landscape. And again, as if to discourage me, the guide book burst into purple prose. "Suddenly," it said, "one's heart is struck. The silence is sudden and pregnant. Suddenly one discovers, or rediscovers, a beauty of an indescribable quality. Pines rise as far as the horizon, as far as the clouds . . ." and a bellyful of description in the same key. To be precise, Le Lioran is eighteen kilometres from Vic, twenty from Murat, and the auto-rail takes one there.

I was informed that I could take the auto-rail in the morning at ten, and should reach Le Lioran in forty-five minutes; then for the rest of the day I could gaze at the pines. Whether it was or wasn't within the scope of my journey to gape at conifers it was difficult to decide. I am one of those seekers of natural beauty who lack all-round enthusiasm. A lake, a river, the oaks of Suffolk or the arid wastes of Cyprus fill me with joy. Mountains do not. Therefore, because perhaps I feel I am missing something, I go to mountains as one might go to see new paintings

177

of a certain school which hitherto failed to impress one.

At any rate, I turned up at the station, bought my ticket to Murat and said in passing I would break my journey at Le Lioran. "Not today," said the stationmaster. "There is no auto-rail this evening from Le Lioran to Murat. You'd have to stay the night."

I could have changed my plans and stayed for the night, but it was such a conscience-soothing excuse that I grasped it. The auto-rail arrived, I got in, soon we reached the first tunnel, then went through several tunnels, short tunnels, which apparently were preparing the traveller for the large tunnel before Le Lioran.

Two gendarmes slept beside me. Forty-two schoolgirls were going on a picnic to Le Lioran. They were between sixteen and seventeen. Twenty-six of them had blue eyes and fair hair. The rest were sallow-faced with black hair and black eyes. They were gay and noisy, imbued with the passionate relationship of giggles and embraces which in a year or so would turn into calf love for the first man who would appear—or has already appeared. I was attracted by an elderly man and his elderly wife. They were out for a picnic too. She opened several times the paper bag containing the sandwiches. She examined them; at intervals she lifted the sandwiches to see whether the ham was still in place. In a hamper were cheese, bread, fruit and a bottle of wine. She checked continuously, touched the cork to make sure it wouldn't pop out, took out the oranges and bananas only to put them back. Then it was the turn of the sandwiches again. Her husband had a short grey beard and a white moustache, yellow above the upper lip. He was above food—for the moment at least. He pointed out the mountains to his wife, and she, with her mind elsewhere, looked obediently at the mountains, repeated the names of the mountains, then sank back to her worries. The husband became rightly excited by a frozen stream hanging on the side of a mountain, a truant caught in time. There were enough pines to make one feel that Le Lioran could have little more to offer. And the auto-rail was mounting. At last came the famous tunnel. The lights came on, and the wife fondled the food anxiously, as if the darkness outside would harm it. The husband, on the other hand, was proud; for he had brought her to the tunnel. It took about a quarter of an hour to reach the other end of the tunnel. Even if comparisons are odious, it wasn't a tunnel of extraordinary length.

The train stopped at Le Lioran, the wife and husband got out, the schoolgirls laughed and shrieked their way out, and the gendarmes slept on. I saw the restaurant near the station where I should have lunched with the warning that I should order my meal a good hour before, as nobody was in a hurry at Le Lioran. I appreciated that: the season begins only when the snow becomes thick.

Through a railway window it is difficult to estimate the height of the sky which the pines were supposed to reach. All I saw was an array of pines and they reached as high as the window permitted. It looked a forlorn spot, and like the tunnel overrated. The auto-rail pulled out. I had no regrets. The enthusiastic guide book states that Le Lioran is prettier in winter. Possibly that is so.

A short man sat down beside me. He was incredibly short. One could have classed him as a dwarf but for the fact that he had none of a dwarf's characteristics, nor the figure. He was a miniature man. He was eager to chat; in fact, he first eyed the gendarmes longingly, speculatively, but they were too deep in sleep, so he gave them up as a hopeless job. It became my turn. He had the sort of moustache film stars fancied in the thirties. The face was pale, the eyes were those of an unsuccessful lady-killer.

"Tomorrow," he said to me, "I'll be back in Paris." I nodded, because I was facing a statement. I couldn't very well say that tomorrow he wouldn't be back in Paris. "And," he went on with a hand on each knee, the shoes not reaching the floor of the carriage, "I will be glad to be out of it." I nodded. "Yes, monsieur, out of it." He mused for a few seconds. "Out of Auvergne, and a very good job. I will be glad. My grandfather was right."

That put me once more into the position of being unable to answer him. His grandfather was right. Granted, as they say, but what was he right about? To ask might be a slur on his grandfather's memory. The gendarmes snored on and we were approaching Murat.

"My grandfather, monsieur," said the excessively short man, "was right. I didn't believe him. My grandfather, alas, died before I was born." It was the same as before. The grandfather had died before he was born, and if I didn't accept that as a fact I would insinuate he, the grandson, was a liar. "My father was seventy-two when I was born. So you can see for yourself."

"Certainly I can," I said, glad I could assure him that I was listening.

"Here we are," he said as the auto-rail stopped at Murat.

"Here we are," I said, and thought that with that repartee our conversation had reached its end.

I decided to leave my luggage at the station. It seemed quite likely that no hotel at Murat would give me the primitive comfort for which I was thirsting. But it wasn't easy to find anybody to whom I could entrust my luggage: the moment the auto-rail pulled out the station fell asleep. Not a soul about, and I waited for a while; then at last a

man, vaguely resembling a railway employee, came out of
the lavatory. I asked him if I could leave my luggage in the
cloakroom. He intimated there was no reason why I
shouldn't but he had nothing to do with the cloakroom.
He made purposeful movements and was ready to walk
away; and nobody in sight; I begged him not to leave me,
and he surrendered to pity.

"But," he said, "don't make a practice of this. I'll do it
this time but only as a favour."

I promised not to do it again. He took my luggage, I
tipped him, he said it would be in the cloakroom, the
cloakroom attendant would soon be back. I came out of the
station and there was a shunting yard to the right and a
row of hastily pulled up houses to the left. It was warm,
and one of the cheap new houses displayed the legend
Hôtel-Bar-Restaurant. I went in, a few railway workers
were sitting at a table, I moved to the bar and before I could
order a drink a voice said: "So here you are." It was the
miniature man.

"So here I am," I said. Would it always go on like that?

"What will you drink?" he asked.

"White wine," I said, and for the barmaid the deep
voice from under the counter, as it were, must have
sounded as a command from the nether world. The bar was
high, and while we chatted he stood against the bar as a
solitary, cornered fighter stands against a wall. He was,
however, so well proportioned that his lack of height never
became entirely obvious. It wouldn't have occurred to me
to hand him his glass notwithstanding that the top of the
bar was almost out of his reach. I let him struggle without
being aware of it.

"Monsieur," he said, "my grandfather was right. I
should explain to you why my grandfather was right. I
liked you at once, if you permit me to say so."

"That's very flattering," I said. I couldn't help reflecting that if the gendarmes had been awake he wouldn't have spoken to me.

"My grandfather was a great traveller. He travelled far and wide. He went to Alsace, and he went to Switzerland, and once he went even to Baden-Baden, and," he dropped his voice, "he came even to Auvergne. Yes, Auvergne. I followed in his footsteps and reached the same conclusions. Nearly a hundred years later. Just think of that."

"I'm trying to," I said. He looked at me triumphantly. "Very remarkable," I added.

"My grandfather reached the conclusion," he went on, "that this is the most God-forsaken land in the world. I am from the Nièvre, my grandfather was from the Nièvre. We have a family estate in the Nièvre. Monsieur, this is the most God-forsaken land in the world."

"But very beautiful."

"Monsieur, I am not willing to argue, besides you have two opinions against you: my grandfather's and mine. I simply told you what my grandfather said, and what his grandson says. I should like to point out to you that my grandfather kept a travel diary."

That was final; for a travel journal couldn't be wrong. If the journal said Auvergne wasn't beautiful, then nothing more could be said on the subject. So I decided to keep my opinion to myself. Besides, he didn't need it. He stared at the bar wall, then turned back to me.

"My grandfather," he said, "saw wolves in this inhospitable country. Wolves." He said wolves as if only Auvergne had ever possessed those pests, in fact as if Auvergne had invented wolves in order to make the traveller feel less secure.

"He saw them," he said, "he saw them everywhere. Once the horses of the carriage in which he travelled bolted. Why? Wolves, monsieur. My grandfather nearly fell out. Incidentally, monsieur, it was a hired carriage, and the coachman tried to cheat him. He charged him much too much.''

He waited. There was a lot I could have said, but I just nodded, waiting for him to go on, which was, after all, his intention.

"He found the inns dirty," he said. "Clermont was a dirty town, Riom a dirty village. I won't mention the Cantal because he was so shocked by what he saw that he cut his journey short. It's all in his journal. Then, monsieur," he said, raising his voice, "there were eagles. My grandfather saw them. You will, whatever you feel about it, agree with me that what with wolves, eagles, a coachman who cheats, one can't blame my grandfather for having cut his journey short. But you can find other memorable items in my grandfather's journal. My grandfather wasn't finicky. He was a bachelor, a gay, carefree bachelor in those days. Well, monsieur, in Clermont he had an unpleasant adventure. Unpleasant? Unpleasant is hardly the word. That adventure was of a very private nature, and so it isn't for me to disclose it. A so-called *jeune fille*. You hear me?''

"Yes. A so-called *jeune fille*.''

"Guess, monsieur," he said.

"I guess.''

"A so-called *jeune fille*. In Clermont. Clermont, as we all know, is in Auvergne. Auvergne." He dropped his voice to a hissing whisper of disgust. "Auvergne.'' Then to my surprise he said he hoped I wasn't an Auvergnat. I assured him I wasn't, and it was my turn to ask him why he had come to Murat.

"I'm following in my grandfather's footsteps," he said. "He came to Murat, stayed for two days. I am here only till noon." He nodded vigorously. "My grandfather saw a wolf quite near here. He was travelling from Saint-Flour to this town. From childhood onward I was determined to follow in his footsteps, but never had time to do so. Now at last . . .'' He had a coughing fit, spat, then took out his handkerchief as an afterthought. ''I owe it, if you understand, to my grandfather's shades.''

''How long will this pilgrimage take you?''

''Three days. Today is the second day. Tomorrow I'm off to Clermont.''

''You should be careful,'' I said, but he didn't see my point.

There are moments when one knows that all one can get out of a person in the way of conversation has been lavishly given to one, and to linger would mean a waste of time. Therefore I told him that somebody was waiting for me, and left. I looked back from the door: he was purposefully approaching the railway workers.

Already from the auto-rail I had noticed the Roc of Bonnevie on top of which stands the statue of Our Lady of Haute Auvergne. It dates from the beginning of this century, and whether it is or isn't a good work of sculpture it is impossible to decide from the distance; but it is well sited and dominates the town. The river Allagnon flows past the town, the town is in fact in the valley of the Allagnon. I could hardly visualise any more a town without a river. The towns of the Cantal are old houses beside a river.

I walked into the town through an abominable street flanked by cheaply built new houses, then I was in the square and soon in the old town consisting of narrow, mounting streets and houses built of basalt, the streets leading to the church.

According to legend Murat was a Celtic colony, and to Murat came St. Mamet in the first century. In Celtic Murat means a steep rock. Now comes a huge leap in time.

Murat

Saint-Flour from the Hill

La Bourrée: the Dance of Auvergne

The English sacked Murat in 1337 but never took the castle. In the reign of Charles VII (somehow Charles VII always comes into the picture) Murat sent soldiers to help the king to rid the country of the English. François I gave Murat to his mother, Louise de Savoie, and in 1531 it was united with the Crown of France. During the Revolution Murat, like most of the towns of the Cantal, showed little fanaticism. Churches were closed, priests, monks and nuns expelled, and with that the good citizens felt they had done their duty. The Revolution fundamentally left no deep impression on Auvergne. If one wishes to indulge in fancies, one could say that Cardinal de Richelieu, who had neither the blood nor the traditions of the feudal oligarchy, had calmed the Revolution in Auvergne in advance by having the castles of the great nobles demolished.

In Murat was born Jean de l'Hôpital, doctor to the Connétable de Bourbon and father of the Chancellier de l'Hôpital, and a whole crop of famous physicians hail from Murat too, including Guillaume and Jean de Travers, the latter the medical attendant of Louis XI, Pierre de Béral, doctor of Henri IV, Pierre-Hugues de Béral, the doctor of Louis XII. Murat had suffered the hell of the German occupation. Houses were burned down, and one hundred and seventeen hostages were taken in 1944, one hundred of them perishing in concentration camps. The Germans must have considered that a pleasing round figure.

With that bit of a bird's-eye view of local history in mind, I walked up the streets, which were busy and full of sunshine. I remembered that in Vic they had said the tunnel of Le Lioran separated the Midi from the France of which Paris was the centre. To be frank, the only difference I noticed on this side of the tunnel was the name of a butcher-shop. It was called Boucherie Parisienne. But the people seemed more gay, that is less morose-looking, than on the other side of the tunnel. If I compared it with Aurillac it was definitely a cheerful town. There was a great deal of coming and going in the narrow, mounting streets. Now and then a lorry appeared, and I had to seek refuge in a doorway or a shop, for the street was hardly wide enough for the lorry. I saw a few hens and couldn't quite make out where they lived. I reached the church.

The original church had been struck by lightning in 1493, burned down, only the black Virgin, albeit in wood, wasn't caught by the flames. That black Virgin is Nôtre-Dame-des-Oliviers. The church was rebuilt by the order of Anne of Austria, who was Vicomtesse of Murat. The statue of Our Lady is robed in gold, and the Infant Christ is robed in gold too. The Child Jesus holds out His hand. Next to the Virgin of Roc-Amadour the Virgin of Murat moved me the most. It used to be thought that the statue had been brought back by St. Louis from the Holy Land. It had been proved, however, that it belongs to the French art of the fifteenth century. That was proved chiefly by the fact that the Oriental Virgins were sculpted sitting on a throne—Nôtre-Dame-des-Oliviers is standing up. Behind me in the church two old women carried on in a whisper a long, angry conversation. I couldn't help glancing at them. They had the rapacious faces of those who had taken faith too long and too easily for granted. They were speaking in patois, so I couldn't understand what they were saying, but, to judge by their expression, it was either slanderous gossip or they were discussing the price of eggs. As I left the church they gave me angry looks. I was the intruder. At the door I ran into a third old woman with little charity showing in her bearing and features. She went up to the other two women and added her angry whispers to theirs.

I took a street which mounted steeply, then turned to the right, then took a street to the left, and I was straight

back in the street through which I had approached the
church. In a strange town one has, unfortunately, only one
street. It is like the *querencia* of a bull in the ring. I have
been to towns where I wanted to explore everything, but
whichever way I turned I found myself irrevocably in the
first street I had encountered on my arrival.

So I didn't look for new streets but took myself back to
the square. I went to a café with red chairs and red tables.
I sat down on the terrace. If I had stayed on in Murat, I
should certainly have gone back to that café every day
simply because it was my first café in the town, though
there were three more cafés in the square. One street, one
café, and thus it goes.

Two peasants sat at the next table in black suits, and,
surprisingly enough, they laughed a good deal. Three young
men, who looked like clerks, chattered gaily, and there was
no inflection of rancour in their voices. A thin man sat
farther on in the company of a fat woman who wore a hat
of the colour of the chairs and the tables. I had the sudden,
far from displeasing sensation that I was out of the jungle.
There I was wrong.

The square was alive, buses came and went, a fat horse
pulled a small cart, facing the café was a car park with little
old cars parked side by side, and as the hour of the soup
was at hand, the cars started up, the café became empty,
and I decided not to move on to Saint-Flour but stay the
night. I asked the waiter which was the best hotel in town.
He gave me the name of an hotel that wasn't far from the
station. I was in high fettle and dearly loved Auvergne.

My love of Auvergne left me when I reached the hotel.
A man and a woman were on and off behind the bar. At my
entrance they happened both to be there and eyed me dis-
approvingly. It was the same as it had been everywhere else.
I was trespassing in order to let them earn their living.

Whatever one thinks or feels about the French, it must be admitted that the Frenchman and the Frenchwoman work hard for their money. They have no sense of class guilt even if they do the humblest of jobs, and they perform them with admirable industry. If a Frenchman or a French-woman runs an hotel, it is run civilly, efficiently, and it is understood that the client pays and the hotel-keeper does all he can to please him. The Auvergnat disapproves of that convention. The hotel at Murat was a blatant proof of that. I asked for a drink: it took their time in coming. I was given the wrong drink. I pointed out I hadn't ordered that drink. They looked offended, nothing happened, eventually the woman said to the man the drink was probably for somebody in the dining-room. They both went with the drink to the dining-room. I was left alone for about ten minutes. A young man, who had come a little earlier, turned to me and spoke in English. That was the first bit of English, though not fluent, I had heard since I jumped into the jungle.

"These people haves no ideas to serving," he said.

Thus our friendship began. He told me, because he was anxious to talk of himself, that he was the representative of an American firm of cosmetics. He had little to do with America: he was, as it were, under the orders of the English branch. He had been to Bournemouth the year before. He thought Bournemouth was a town of exceptional beauty. I hazarded a question: did he like English cooking?

"Bacon and eggs," he said. "I adore them. And kippers. Oh, kippers."

His eyes shone. Then he spoke with passion of shep-herd's pie. He said there was nothing like it in France. I said that was one of the chief reasons why I came so often to France. He was an enchanting young man.

The woman came back, I asked for the drink I had

ordered. I was served, the young man insisted on paying
and continued to praise Bournemouth and shepherd's pie,
though by then I had succeeded in making him praise them
in French. I asked the woman after another of her absences
whether I could lunch at the hotel. She considered that a
question not quite worthy of an answer. The young man
said he would lunch too, then suggested we should eat
together. After the many solitary meals I had had I jumped
at it, and said: with pleasure. The woman intensely disliked
the idea. At the end of the luncheon I found out why. The
young man and I went into the dining-room, which was
full to capacity. There was no bill of fare: food was put
before one and one had to like it. As a matter of fact, it was
easy to like it because it was good food. The waitress
succeeded in being as disagreeable as apparently she wished
to be.

During luncheon the young man spoke of interesting
matters. To my surprise he did good business with cosmetics in Auvergne. Peasant women? He assured me he
did well with peasant women. There was, admittedly,
sales resistance in places, but he got round it because he was
pleasant and good-looking. His strongest weapon was to
make up their faces without charging anything.

"In Auvergne," he laughed, "nobody can resist anything
that is free."

He had gone to a special school, as he put it, with other
representatives of the firm, to learn how to make up a
woman's face. He could do it as well as any ladies' hairdresser. He would, he explained, go to a farm; the husband
was usually out in the fields, so he could play on the
woman's vanity by using his charm. The woman wouldn't
hear of it at first: no, certainly not, she had never been made
up, her face was the face of a healthy, decent woman, and a
lot more in the same vein. The prettier they were the easier

they fell. I said I thought it would be the other way round. Then I thought it over and saw his point. It is always more difficult to convince the desperate. He would tell the woman that her beauty could but improve with make-up, and slightly flirtatious yet respectful, he would persuade her to give him a chance. Nine times out of ten the woman was delighted with her new face and bought cosmetics.

"I don't know," he said, "what the husbands think when they come home. But I have no business with husbands."

It was towards the end of our luncheon that he proposed to drive me in his car to Saint-Flour. He would have to visit two villages on the way, but would reach Saint-Flour by the evening. I accepted gratefully. He asked for our bills, which created confusion. The maid blushed, looked at me, then at him, eventually my bill was brought to me, and he was asked to go and see the woman in the bar. I waited for him and when he returned he explained that as a commercial traveller he was entitled to a reduction, and the woman had been afraid that if I saw him paying less I would object to my bill. The Auvergnat, certainly, thinks of everything.

The young man drove a Simca. He explained that the car was bought by the firm, and he paid it off in instalments. Things didn't go smoothly at the station. Nobody could find my luggage. After a while a man came in shirtsleeves and told me firmly that it was no business of his. Furthermore, he hadn't the key of the cloakroom. There was a train towards six o'clock and the man who had the key was bound to turn up for that train. He was rolling a cigarette, the interview was over, and I knew that the young man would leave without me because he had, naturally enough, his time schedule. Small misfortunes can drive one easily to despair; big catastrophes are often above despair.

The young man was waiting in his car: at that moment I had but one wish, one desire in life, namely to travel with the young man in the Simca. High treason would have been a cheap price for it. I left the man in shirt-sleeves, moving despondently in the direction of the Simca, and suddenly I saw my luggage outside the station beside a door of the station building. Evidently nobody had bothered to put it into the cloakroom, and there it was for anyone to take. My joy was boundless.

We drove out of Murat, and from then onward everything began to move at breakneck speed, as though Auvergne, tired of my critical mind, wanted to shake me off. The young man drove dangerously. He took corners on the wrong side of the turning, overtook cars where there was practically no room, hooted continuously, as if hooting could save us from violent death, talked and boasted; for he had reached the stage of a young man's chat where success with women becomes the sole topic. An exceedingly rich half-caste woman was in love with him, she was twenty years older than he, and she would do anything in the world for him both with her body and her purse. He admired her purse.

"Look out," I cried.

"I am a good driver."

He turned moody, and speculated on the advantages and miseries marrying for money involved. It was the reverie of a man whose mind seemed already made up. Should he or shouldn't he sacrifice himself for lucre? We left the main road, and after we had pirouetted round a hairpin bend I saw lava, lava left over by burning Auvergne, the lava of which all books I had read on Auvergne spoke eloquently.

"Is this lava?" I asked.

"I don't know. I'm only twenty-seven. Should one throw away one's life for money at so early an age?"

"One shouldn't. Is this lava?"

"I see what you mean. I might go into business with her money and then, if I am rich enough, I could leave her, if you see my point."

Perhaps it wasn't lava. The road twisted, but all roads twist in the Cantal, and we rushed past a waterfall, sheep were grazing in a valley, and we reached a village. The village was more than a village though not yet a town. It belonged to the pattern I had got accustomed to. The church was of the fourteenth century, rebuilt at the end of the last, the houses were grey, with a few cheap modern houses breaking the grey line, the cafés dark and mostly empty, and plenty of cow dung in the street. Lorries were parked not near enough to the curb, and one could hardly drive past them.

The young man left me outside a café and went to a hairdresser across the road. I ordered a glass of red wine and waited. A few children stared at me, found me an unexciting sight and moved on. Neither the café-keeper nor his womenfolk, of whom there was a fair number, took any notice of me. The young man came back in a bad temper. The hairdresser was a fool, a bumpkin, a cuckold, in short he wanted no cosmetics. The young man sat down, took a list of names from his brief case, and found out he had gone to the wrong hairdresser. The hairdresser across the road was no client of his firm.

"Stay here," he said. "I'm going to my client. I will be back in half an hour."

He drove off and then a shameful thing happened. As he let in the clutch I was bowled over by unworthy suspicion. I became convinced that the kind young man who had given me a lift out of the kindness of his heart, was off with my luggage, and I would never see him again. He would sell my suits, shirts and shoes, and I should be left high and dry in the village covered with cow dung. I felt covered with cow dung too. I saw myself alerting the entire police of the Cantal. I sat, waited, and distrust was my master. It seemed entirely plausible that he would act as I feared. The half-hour went by and there was no young man. Why should there be? He was busy selling. There was a tie in one of my suitcases to which I was particularly attached. I nearly sobbed thinking of that tie. I walked up and down in the street, whenever I heard a car I turned round, but it wasn't the Simca. I walked as far as a jeweller, and stared at cheap watches, engagement rings and clocks in wooden cases, and then I heard another car. There was the young man. He had done well, his client had ordered a lot of cosmetics. I asked him to have a drink, he said it was too hot, I pestered him, finally forcing a brandy on him simply to ease my guilty, blushing conscience.

We drove on, crossed a main road. New mountains were rising in the distance. To date all the mountains I had seen in Auvergne were, so to speak, in the shadow of the Puy-Mary. The landscape now began to shift towards the Puy du Dôme. There are expressions patented by guide books. Smiling valleys, laughing rivers, and the adjectives can be changed round. So we saw laughing valleys, smiling rivers, and the young man giggled a good deal. He was back to his favourite subject: the rich woman who wished to marry him. He gave me one or two scabrous details of their love life. I couldn't help wondering what he would feel like if he married her and ran into me with her at his side. But probably by then he would have forgotten that he had given me those intimate tales of their bedchamber. He stopped in a tiny village. He had to call on a man who lived a few houses away from the only inn. That man owned scent shops in many parts of Auvergne, so he had to keep in with him. He wouldn't be long and left the car before the inn. Thus I couldn't let myself down again by not trusting him.

The inn was dark, cool and had no bar. Two long tables were in the middle, a few chairs against the wall, and an old woman brought me a glass of wine. She did not ask, but stated that I was a Parisian. She spoke French with some difficulty. I sat down, she stood beside me and talked. She was the daughter of a peasant, her husband had been a peasant, and though above military age in 1914, he had gone to the war.

"They say of us Auvergnats," she said, "that we don't love France. We love France more than the French do. Look at my husband. He was killed for France, and God alone knows how much we needed him on the farm. I had to work very hard, and when the war was over I had the idea of starting this inn. It helps, and now I am too old to work on the land."

I watched her thinking. She must have felt lonely when I came in, or possibly she had spoken of her past troubles so much to the villagers that they had no desire left to listen to her. She was visibly thinking, for she was determined to talk. A vacant look in her eyes gave me the impression that she had suddenly nothing more left to say about herself. That was understandable. One hoards it and discusses it so often with oneself that by the time the chance comes to give it away, most of it remains on the other side of the blocked channel connecting the brain with the tongue.

"You people, monsieur," she burst out, "don't appreciate us the Auvergnats. I spoke here the other day to a very learned man from Paris. He said we don't laugh and don't like strangers. That isn't true. We have lived so much alone and, as I once read it in a paper, when strangers came in the old days they came with no good intentions. Besides, we are very busy and have no time for empty politeness.

Scraping and bowing are for those who have little else to do." She became a little anxious because I might be one of those who spend their time scraping and bowing, in which case she had offended me. "If monsieur doesn't agree he should say so. Every argument has two sides."

"I suppose you are right," I said. "It's a pity, though, that so few people come to this beautiful country. I have seldom seen such a beautiful land."

That pleased her immensely. She almost had tears in her tired blue eyes. She asked me eagerly which part of the Cantal I had liked most. I said Salers. She was disappointed, and was of the opinion that I would change my mind once I got to Saint-Flour. I asked her whether she knew any of the hotels in Saint-Flour. She said she didn't; when she went to Saint-Flour it was only on market days, and came back in the evening. But she was convinced that there were excellent hotels. Later she told me she hadn't been out of the village for six years. She also told me that the Germans had taken one of her grandsons, who had died in a concentration camp. She sniffed a lot while she told me that. Because it was nearer in time it was more of a loss to her than the death of her husband in the nebulous past. The young man returned.

He was suspiciously gay. We had two glasses of wine, and I reached the correct conclusion that he hadn't a strong head. Driving with him, I feared, would become an even more exceptional experience. The old woman had retired into a shell of silence, and when we left she said goodbye distantly. Thus once more I observed how quickly and easily the cord of intimacy can be cut in Auvergne.

As we drove out of the village a pretty girl in a cotton dress came out of the last house. She was going to cross the road. The young man stopped the car abruptly and leaned out.

"Who makes up that beautiful face of yours, mademoiselle?" he asked. "I'd love to know. You look so ravishing." I blushed; the girl, tossing her head, walked on without saying a word. "Stupid peasant girl," said the young man angrily. "She wasn't even made up, the goose."

He didn't speak any more of his prospective bride. He told me a long story of a girl living in the Haute Loire, whom he fancied. She had black hair, hazel eyes and had a pretty voice. In a day or two he would be in the Haute Loire and see her. He was pleased with the prospect and just missed a lorry.

We bowled into Saint-Flour. The town on top of a rock, surrounded by valleys, with a half-circle of mountains guarding it at a distance, was as impressive a sight as one could ask for. The young man had heard of an hotel in the main square. It was cheap and comfortable. We drove through a narrow street, mounted the pavement to give room to a bus, then came into the square near the cathedral. He put on the brakes. Two women, one of them rather pretty, were in front of the car. First they looked frightened, but fell afterwards under the charm of the young man's smile, which seldom deserted him.

"Where," he asked them, "do you buy your cosmetics? You look ravishing, but you'd look far more ravishing if you let me make up your faces."

The women giggled, they entered into conversation, he got a certain amount of information about the local hairdressers, he said he regretted he wasn't staying the night; would, however, come back quite soon, and then he would seek them out and make their faces radiant with beauty. Good humour and badinage reigned—all that in the middle of the square. We parted on the best of terms—the young man appeared to own a world peopled exclusively with pretty women—and we drove on to the hotel which was next door to the Senate House. He remained in the car: I went in.

I entered an ordinary bistro and there was nobody at the counter. A few men were lolling about, two of them the worse for drink. At last a pleasant man, given to fat, appeared. He was the proprietor and took me upstairs, showed me a dark room, said there was no bathroom, and sanitary arrangements were primitive. There are moments when one gives in to anything, and I, caught by such a moment, nearly said I liked hotels with dark rooms and primitive sanitary arrangements. Anyway, I said I would stay the night. He sang the praises of the food he served. In France an hotel is judged by its food, sanitation and accommodation coming only in the wake of the fare. He was a cheerful man and his talk made me feel hungry.

As I knew that the young man wasn't remaining for the night, I went out to the Simca to ask him in for a farewell drink. He said he had a few hours to waste, therefore he wanted to go and see the viaduct of Garabit, which he called the finest viaduct in France. I loyally riposted that the viaduct of Souillac was the finest viaduct in France, adding I was only too pleased to go with him and make the comparison. We left the old town, drove through the new town, then out to the road and with mountains, dales, cattle and water on each side of the road we drove fast, even faster than before, to the viaduct.

"This," I said when we arrived, "is the Eiffel Tower horizontally."

"There's something in that," said the young man.

I wasn't wrong. The viaduct was built in 1882 according to the plans of Eiffel. The viaduct is five hundred and sixty-four metres long, but such figures mean little to me. It looked like a brave piece of engineering. I had the good luck to see a train crossing it, which brought it alive far more than the figures concerning height, span and God alone knows what.

The young man was enthralled. To him the steel contraption meant more than a Romanesque church or a Renaissance house. He said that was civilisation, that was true beauty, and he could have admired it for hours. Near the viaduct was an hotel; we went and sat on the hotel terrace. The young man's eyes remained glued to the viaduct, he drank now as fast as was his habit to drive, and clouds were gathering above the wooded hills. He complimented himself on having taken the trouble to visit the viaduct. He was the pilgrim satisfied with the pilgrimage.

To me the viaduct seemed a Pyrrhic victory. Those who had planned it and built it could have built something simpler and less complicated from the engineering point of view. To span that chasm they had easier means at their disposal. But no; in the name of progress they built that horizontal Eiffel Tower, built it to the glory of the all-conquering industrial age, as churches had been built in the past to the glory of God. A few more such feats, they must have thought, and the millennium of material triumph would descend on earth. Yet in a comparatively short time they were superseded, outdistanced, and their faith and enthusiasm are no longer appreciated. Progress gave them joy but no suspicion. So how could they be understood today? The young man turned to me.

"Those who built that viaduct," he said, "must have thought they were on their way to conquer the world. Look, just look. Something entirely different has conquered the world."

"It is just an historical monument," I said. "The Ministère des Beaux Arts should take it under its protection."

The young man laughed, then had another drink. I was becoming worried. From behind the new range of mountains a bevy of clouds was advancing. The young man wanted to order another round of drinks, but I insisted on returning to Saint-Flour.

"Perhaps you are afraid of thunder," he said.

"That's it," I said. "Terribly afraid."

Nobody in fear of thunder could have been more afraid than I was during our drive back to Saint-Flour. The rain came down, we reached Saint-Flour, and I relaxed, and then I knew that I couldn't spend the night in the dark room near the Senate House. The young man said there was a more luxurious hotel. We decided to try that. The young man left me in the car and went in to inquire about prices. The hotel was in a large square in which a circus had performed recently. The square was more or less derelict land.

The young man came back from the hotel, said room and board were about a thousand francs a day, but I should go in myself and speak to the proprietor, which I did. The proprietor in appearance reminded me of the usual type of Auvergnat one finds in Paris, either a restaurateur or a coal merchant. We haggled for a while. I was talking to no simple child of the Cantal: he owned an hotel in Paris too, and haggling was on his fingertips. We looked at rooms, and on the threshold of every room the price of the room was discussed. He was a heavy man, innocent of smiles. Nothing on this earth, his countenance betrayed, could amuse him. From the windows the view was of rare majesty. The hotel was situated on the edge of the steep rock on which rested the old town. There was a straight drop of several hundred feet; on the other side of the valley the mountains stood sombre in the rain. He spoke vigorously of the cash value of the view. After a fair amount of bargaining I chose a room and the price was agreed on. I would pay for room, dinner, breakfast and luncheon twelve hundred francs. It was raining cats and dogs, the clouds sat on the town, yet the clouds lighted from behind by the invisible sun had a furious appearance.

I went to the bar where the young man was waiting for me. He had become heavy with drink; nevertheless, the prospect of seeing the girl in the Haute Loire gave his heaviness a lyrical sting. He chatted of her, described her prowess in bed, and the rich woman wasn't even mentioned. I have a good memory, so I couldn't help asking him where the rich woman fitted in.

"She," he said. "Oh, I invented the whole thing. I don't know any rich woman. Do you suppose I'd be selling cosmetics in these stinking towns if I could get hold of a rich woman?"

"Of course not," I said politely.

"There you are."

Soon afterwards he left. We said goodbye; I promised to contact him on my return to Paris, and our parting was effusive. I suppose he forgot me by the next morning, and by the time I reached Paris he was turfed out of my memory. All the same, we parted like friends who can't live without each other; and that is a nice way to part.

It rained and I saw no reason to go out. The hotel proprietor was behind the bar, talking to two men sitting at a table. He was called away, and one of the men cheered me up by remarking he robbed his clients without shame. I said he might do one, but that was no concern of mine; for we had agreed in advance on the price. A little later I went to the dining-room. I didn't care for it. I have possibly spent more time in restaurants than most people; especially in France, a country I have frequented regularly from childhood onward, yet I have seldom had a house or a flat,

Saint-Flour: the Ramparts

Saint-Flour: Old Houses

The Viaduct of Garabit

The Rocks of Saint-Flour

hence restaurants became synonymous with the daily necessity of feeding. Consequently I am acquainted with restaurants of different categories, and I can, as it were, smell the price, the cooking and the proprietor's attitude towards honesty the moment I come in. That restaurant had a strong smell of dishonesty. The wrought-iron lamps and polished copper saucepans strengthened that smell. The bill of fare was also dishonest. Ordinary workaday dishes were proudly presented as local specialities—one should beware of that word. I ordered hot sausage. It was a small, anaemic sausage, a sausage I could have eaten anywhere: nevertheless, it was classed as a speciality. I was the only guest in the dining-room. A woman with a long unpleasant face and too many teeth sat behind a desk near the door. Her disapproving look kept me company during dinner. I was glad to go to bed. I believe I was alone in the hotel. The monotonous sound of dropping rain was all I heard.

Saint-Flour was built on a basaltic rock which is nine hundred metres high. The origins of the town go back to Sr. Flour, who was a disciple of Our Lord. In the Middle Ages the town had about seven thousand inhabitants; nowadays the population is only four thousand. During the two Hundred Years' Wars, while the English occupied Guyenne, Saint-Flour was a frontier town. Charles VII, it is almost superfluous to add, visited the town twice. In the course of the Wars of Religion, Capitaine Merle, renowned for his sardonic cruelty, attacked the town in force one night. Jean Brisson, one of the consuls, heard the enemy approaching, alerted the town and Merle was repulsed. Only the wind, so they boast locally, has ever conquered Saint-Flour. The town was the birthplace of some famous physician and of Belloy the actor. Undoubtedly Auvergne has contributed more than her share

to the French medical profession. Saint-Flour is a bishop-
ric. Some of the bishops were famous men in their days. In
feudal times among the bishops one finds the most powerful
names of Auvergne.

I sat up in bed, read the notes I had made and perceived I
wasn't interested in the history of Saint-Flour. Too many
towns in too short a time with too much history, I said to
myself. I should at least look up the name of the famous
physician. I couldn't be bothered and fell asleep.

I woke in the morning to the sound of rain. Somehow I
remembered a morning in Windsor at the beginning of
March. It was raining, steadily, gloomily, the Castle wet
and sad in the rain. I went to a tobacconist, and he said
while he served me the rain would never stop. To cap him
I replied flippantly: "Don't you know there will be no
summer this year?" I thought ruefully of my remark as
I opened the shutters. I looked down into the valley. The
rain fell into the valley; a lorry was coming up the road, the
water of the puddles like foam in front of the radiator. A
dismal doom seemed to permeate the view. I wasn't pleased.
I had looked forward to my visit to Saint-Flour. Several
years ago I had seen a poster of the town in a tourist agency.
The cathedral, the rock with the town on top of it, the
river in the valley, the mountains behind, and now there
was only the grey wall of rain. A man was driving a few wet
sheep along the road in the valley. I felt sorry for the sheep,
the shepherd, and the postman bicycling behind them. I had
a tepid bath: the water wasn't hot. I breakfasted in the
dining-room, and the cashier eyed me with lack of favour
again. A man and a woman were at the next table, both
complaining bitterly of the rain. I mentioned to the cashier
that the water hadn't been warm.

"It is warm," she said.

Rain or no rain, I was going to see the town. I went out

and soon the rain stopped. The interval; and new clouds were coming up.

In the Place d'Armes had stood in days gone by a bronze statue of Christ. The sculptor had made a hole in the side of the statue—the hole made by the lance of the Roman soldier. In Saint-Flour the wind is a hard master, and the wind entering the hole produced a lugubrious yet sinister sound. In fact, the statue moaned. What became of the statue I do not know.

The Cathedral is Gothic, austere both outside and inside. Of the original Romanesque church the sacristy alone remains. I felt like agreeing with Prosper Mérimée, who said of the façade it lacks nobility and gives the impression of a lay building. The towers belong to no known style of architecture, and he considered them detestable. But from the distance they are quite imposing. I much admired the Crucifix with the black Christ. It is of the fifteenth century, and is known as the Bon Dieu de Saint-Flour. The cathedral had its share of chattering old women, and their voices accompanied me as I moved about. It was raining again outside.

To the right of the cathedral is the mairie. It used to be the bishop's palace, but when the Church was disestablished in 1905 it was taken over by the state. The palace had been built by Charles de Noailles, Bishop of Saint-Flour and abbé of Aurillac. It is an admirable building. The other outstanding building in the square is the Maison Consulaire. In that house had lived the consul who had saved the town from Merle. I should have liked to visit the house. The Syndicat was in the square. I repaired there with scant hope: I left with none. A charming young girl received me. I asked whether it was possible to visit the house. She said it was out of the question. It belonged to somebody or other, she didn't know the person's name, and she was sorry but she couldn't help. They had small printed maps of the town. Would I like one? I asked her a few questions. She shook her attractive head and said she didn't know. She said that gently: it was a friendly rebuke. I felt as if I had gone to a chemist and wanted to buy a tie.

I took myself to the ramparts and looked down. With the new town to the right, the bridges, the mountains, the woods and pastures, the view was as soothing yet as spectacular as Auvergne alone can provide. An old man came out of a house built probably at the beginning of the seventeenth century, took a long document from his pocket, read it, put it back into his pocket, spat and returned to the house. An old woman came puffing up a narrow muddy path. Otherwise the town seemed altogether lifeless.

Accompanied by a few raindrops I walked along the rue de Belloy, then followed the rue Sorel, and in the Place de la Halle is the flamboyant Gothic church of Nôtre-Dame. At the present time it is used for storing wheat. Even though it is no longer a church, even though it is used for utilitarian purposes, I found it impressive; and the raindrops became heavier. Soon I was back on the ramparts, and gazed at the new town, vulgar and ugly even in the distance. None the less, it fascinated me. Since I had entered Auvergne I was surrounded by and in the midst of Romanesque churches, waterfalls, valleys, Renaissance houses and red cattle. The world in which, whether for better or worse, all the same one lives, had gone from me. The new town with a few factory chimneys, tenements, garages, in brief the bag of tricks of present-day existence, beckoned to me, much to my annoyance and surprise. It was as though the life I had led for the last fortnight was unreal; not for me; but down there with railway station, goods trains and lorries was what I was searching for. Not Charles VII, but a wooden barrack housing roadmenders.

I took a narrow, steep path. The path led past old houses, which slowly dropped away. The path was muddy, littered with cow dung, and an old man was nimbly mounting it. "You took a very bad road, monsieur," he said, and I could justly have answered him that in a strange town one is bound to take the wrong or bad road. A narrow stream crossed the path; the clouds were preparing for action; I came down near a butcher's, went past an ironmonger's, and found myself beside a bridge. There was another bridge farther on. I was in the new town, which strikingly resembled the sort of outskirts of Paris at which one gazes with a shudder when one's train is approaching Paris. Mean buildings, small factories and tin shacks. Men went about their business in overalls, lorries sprayed with mud and water the narrow pavement, the shops catered for the poor, and the cafés were small, dark and cheap. And nowhere could I see picture postcards for the tourist. In a curious, almost frightening manner I was enjoying myself. There was a dour sense of reality around me; moreover, I hadn't to stand on my aesthetic tiptoes all the time. I could say ugly and like it. The rain came down and I hurried into a sordid bistro.

Soon the rain covered the street, the new town dwindled, ready to disappear under the impact of the rain. It was dark. A few workmen and a lorry driver were at the counter, an old woman served behind the counter, chatting uninterruptedly with an older woman who sat not far from her. I ordered a drink, and it came home to me that the true reason why I felt at ease was twofold. Firstly, I had ceased to be the traveller, the tourist and the sightseer; if those men in the bistro bothered to give me any thought they would, in all probability, have put me down as a commercial traveller or a factory inspector, but it was more likely they wouldn't bother to put me down as anything.

Secondly, I was outside the terms of reference of this book.
I hadn't been commissioned to write about factory
chimneys, loaded lorries and workmen drinking while waiting to go back to work. I was on holiday from myself and
my pen.

The rain petered out after a little time. I walked on,
listened to the noise of factory machines and railway
engines. No Capitaine Merle, no Cardinal de Richelieu. It
was all infinitely dreary, ugly and soul-killing. Behind me
towered the rock with the old town on its back. The rain
attacked again. I went into another bistro, as dark and
sordid as the one I had left. The rain settled down for the
day. The bistro-keeper was a young man, we were alone,
and he talked on an inept and futile topic, namely what he
would do if he had an hotel in the old town. As he would
probably never have an hotel anywhere, I didn't much listen
to him. It appeared he wouldn't do the tourist, his prices
would be equitable, the food good, drinks inexpensive, even
so he would make a good living and the traveller would be
satisfied.

It was no effort for him to talk in that vein; for there was
no opportunity for him to prove the sincerity of his words.
I nodded, put in a yes here, an I agree with you there, and
the rain slashed the window. Then I became interested. He
was saying it did a lot of harm to the entire town that the
hotel where I was staying overcharged the clients. People
stayed for a day or two, then left the district in disgust.

"But I am staying there," I said. "I'm paying twelve
hundred francs a day. That's not exorbitant."

"I can't believe you. They charge much more."

"I arranged it with the proprietor himself."

"You be careful, that's all I can say."

I didn't like that. The rain fell fast, it was noon, and it
seemed out of the question for the rain, in order to please

me, to cease while I climbed to the old town. I ordered a taxi; the taxi came and drove me back. Not far from the hotel was a bar-tabac. I went there to buy cigarettes, and a middle-aged woman with friendly eyes full of curiosity asked me where I hailed from, did I like Saint-Flour, and at which hotel I stayed. I told her. She shook her head, spoke to the girl who was serving drinks, spoke to her of me as one speaks of a patient in the ward outside in the passage.

"You shouldn't have gone there," she said. "You'll come a cropper as so many others did. You remember the gentleman with his wife and four children last year?" That was to the serving girl. "You remember how much their bill was?" The girl nodded. "And the gentleman refused to pay it and told the proprietor he could sue him."

"That's right," said the maid.

I was far from cheerful. The woman turned her back on me, and said to the wall she was exceedingly sorry for me because I would be fiendishly overcharged. The town suffered because of the high prices at that hotel; in fact, it gave the town a bad name. She hoped I would be luckier than others, but she held out no hope. A couple of men drinking at the counter joined the conversation. As in the days of fairy tales one was warned against the abode of a giant, so I was pitied for having entered the hotel the night before. The woman spoke dramatically to the wall, turned back swiftly to serve a client, the men at the counter advised me to go carefully, watch my step and step out of it as quickly and with as little loss as possible. A woman eating a sandwich at a table joined in. I had become the object of general pity.

"We shall see," I said with little conviction, and went to the hotel.

The cashier was sitting at the desk, the man and woman

who had breakfasted were lunching. I said to the cashier I was leaving and should like to have my bill as arranged the evening before. I had worked it out, after what I heard in the bar-tabac, that it would be preferable to see the bill before I ate. She brought me the bill. It was nineteen hundred francs for the room and the dinner, two hundred more for the cup of coffee I had drunk for breakfast, and the luncheon, luckily not eaten, wasn't included.

"There's a mistake somewhere," I bleated. "I arranged with the proprietor to pay for one's day's pension twelve hundred francs."

"You never made such an arrangement," she said.

"Send for the proprietor."

"The proprietor went to Paris this morning."

"Then send for the proprietress."

She stood up, taking her time over it. The man and the woman at the table were staring at me. I was furious. The proprietress appeared.

"It isn't the custom in this hotel to argue over prices," she said, her voice not only cold but full of disgust. "You suggested to the cashier that you fixed the price with my husband. That's not true. If my husband had made a price for you he would have told me. I know these stories. Please pay the bill at once. The cashier wants to go and eat."

There was a great deal I wanted to say, so all I said was: "When your husband, who is probably skulking in the garden, comes back tell him what I think of him. I leave it to you. Please tell the valet to bring down my luggage."

"The valet is busy," she said.

I paid my bill. I had but one desire, namely to leave the hotel. The cashier took the money and I went back to the bar-tabac. "You were right," I said to the woman.

I listened with satisfaction to the café's opinion of the hotel and its proprietor. It pleased me to hear that he had been seen about before noon. The town, they said, suffered because of his dealings. People came to buy tobacco, and, pointing at me, the dear woman related the story. I remembered I had left my luggage behind. I asked her whether she knew of somebody who would go and and fetch it. Half the bar-tabac went off, and came back with it as if bringing a trophy.

"Are you moving to another hotel?" I was asked.

"No," I said, not surprised by my voice. "I'm leaving. How near can I get to Clermont tonight?"

"At five there's a bus going to Issoire."

"Suits me," I said; and that brought roughly to an end my stay in Auvergne.

Shortly after a red-faced man, wearing spectacles, came in. He had heard of my adventure too. It soon appeared he was the leading optician of Saint-Flour. He apologised in the name of the town, begged me to retain a pleasant memory, and drinks were stood all round and friendship reigned. He invited me to his shop, where he made me the present of some special paper with which to clean my reading glasses. From the shop we went on a triumphal tour through the town, two of his friends accompanying us. We stopped at every bistro and everybody heard my tale of woe. It was no longer my story; it belonged to the optician and his friends. I was slowly pushed out of the picture—that didn't displease me.

The optician was a great talker. He talked of politics. France should be run by the Auvergnats. If they were allowed to run France things would be better; in fact, they would be excellent. His friends agreed with him. It was time for me to take the bus. A pushcart was found, my luggage put into it, and my staunch friends, led by the optician, pushed it to the bus halt. They stayed with me till the bus left. There were hearty handshakes, and wrapt in the cloak of warm friendship I waved goodbye to them. It was only after the excitement of the new camaraderie had slightly worn off that I became aware that I was leaving Auvergne. I regretted my unshakable decision. It had been my intention to finish my journey at the Chaise Dieu. What a fitting end to describe the Chaise Dieu, the monastery and the Dance Macabre. All planned, yet I was on my way to Issoire, tomorrow evening I would be in Paris, and a week later in London.

I could have gone on to the Chaise Dieu from Issoire, but the way I felt, and the fashion in which my mind had been made up, it would have been travelling under false pretences if I had continued on my journey.

I took up a book. It had kept me company from Souillac onward: *A Pilgrimage to Auvergne*, by Louisa Stuart Costello. It was published in 1842. The authoress had had her troubles too; but one can't travel nor enjoy travelling without them. She said of the Auvergnats: "They are a strange wild race, fond of money, avaricious, yet well off, extremely uneducated and coarse in their manners, easily excited, and somewhat brutal in their habits." That was her impression. I, on the other hand, carry pictures away with me. My last picture of Auvergne is the pushcart with my luggage in it, the optician and his friends loyally pushing it. And somehow or other Salers rises in the background, but that is flitting from picture to picture.

"Tomorrow," said a woman beside me to the small child on her knee, "we will be in Clermont. The capital of Auvergne. Do you understand? Our capital."

The child perhaps did: I for one in my mind was already out of Auvergne.

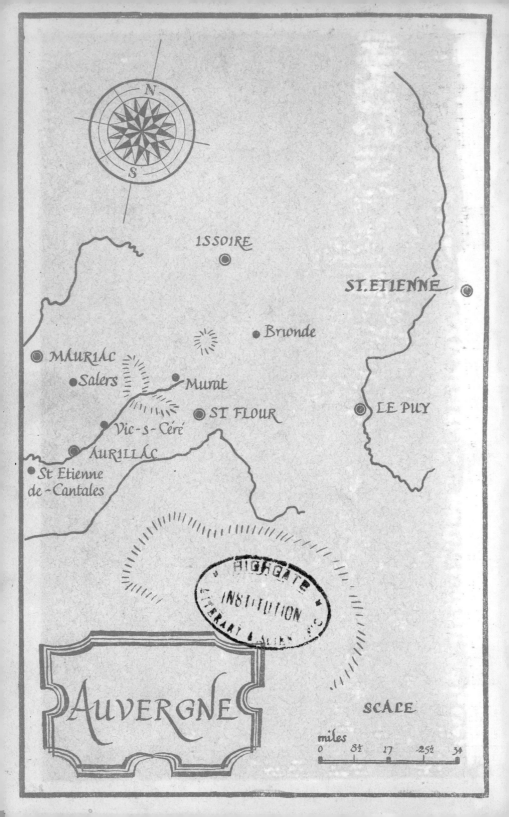

N

S

ISSOIRE

ST. ETIENNE

Brionde

MAURIAC

Salers

Murat

LE PUY

Vic-s-Céré

ST FLOUR

AURILLAC

St Etienne
de - Cantales

AUVERGNE

SCALE

miles

0   8½   17   25½   34